computer graphics

john vince

The Design Council

Published in the United Kingdom in 1992 by
The Design Council
28 Haymarket
London SW1Y 4SU

Printed and bound in Hong Kong
by Dai Nippon Printing Co (HK) Ltd.

The typefaces used in this publication, F.F. Scala, F.F. Meta
and F.F. Marten, are from the Font Font range exclusive to
FontWorks UK Ltd, part of the Fontshop Network.

Cover credits: (front, clockwise from the top) see page 120;
see page 71; see page 10; see page 33; (back) see page 40.

British Library in Publication Data
A catalogue record for this book is available from the
British Library.

ISBN 0 85072 303 5

To Annie, Samantha, Anthony and Ben.

Acknowledgements

Book publishing is a team effort, and although the author is a vital part of this team, they often rely upon professional guidance from the publisher. During the development of this book I have received the continuous support of the Design Council's Publishing Department; in particular, I gratefully acknowledge the invaluable contribution made by the editor, Tracey Williams and the designer, Nicole Griffin.

I would also like to thank the following people and organizations for talking to me about their work and supplying the images for this book.

8vo; Winifred Aldrich, CAD Designer Services; Maggi Allison, The Moving Picture Co; Ampex Corporation; Paul Anscombe, Stuart Cox, Roger Dade and Paul Norris, Bournemouth and Poole College of Art & Design; Phil Baines; Gary Bassin, Twin Planet Communications, Inc; Richard Beer, Scangraphic Visutek Ltd; Paul Biddle; Booth-Clibborn Editions; Mike Boudry, The Computer Film Co; Caroline Brown; Gillian Bunce; Paul Butler; Keith Cass, Independent Television News; Colour Club, Brussels; Dr Brian Collins, IBM UK Scientific Centre; Marilyn Comrie, Crosfield Electronics; Peter Crowther; Charles Csuri; Steve Davidson, Imagination; Sarah Davies, Lambie-Nairn+Company Ltd; Andy Davy, BBC Television; Hazel Dormer, Channel Four News; Annie Eaves, APT Photoset Group; Pam Fisher, Communication Arts; Peter Florence, Cambridge Animation Systems; Liz Friedman, BBC Television; François Garnier, Videosystem; Stephen Ghee, Charles Grimsdale and Clive Jones, Division; John Hamilton; Anna Hart, Hibbert Ralph Animation Ltd; Akira Hasegawa; Pascal Herold, DUPON; Dr Tom Heywood, IBM (UK); Mike Hurst, BSB; IBM European Visualization Centre; Douglas Kay and Lincoln Hu, Industrial Light & Magic; Andrew Johnston, Softimage (UK) Ltd; Jill Jurkowitz, LucasArts Entertainment Co; Siobhan Keaney; Dr Mike King, The City Polytechnic; William Latham and Stephen Todd, IBM UK Scientific Centre; Stephen Lovatt, Canon (UK); Jon McCarthy, EPR Architects Ltd; Stewart McEwan, Electric Image; Cambell McKellar, Thorn EMI Central Research Laboratories; Don Miller; John Murrell, Quantel; Bhash Naidoo, University of Teeside; David Nelson; Paterson Jones Ltd; Debbie Phillips, Courtaulds Socks; PIXELS Aps; Maria Quiroz and David Saunders, Monotype Corporation plc; Sarah Rees and Colin Cheeseman, Ravensbourne College of Design and Communication; Rock Kitchen Harris; Ron Arad Associates Ltd; Royal Mail; Joaquin Rico, Souverein BV; Dr Gordon Selley, Real World Graphics; Graham Shepherd, BBC Television; Kevin Simpson, The Electronic Font Foundry; Brenda Sparkes, Nottingham Polytechnic; Kenneth Snelson; Tim Stimpson, Next Directory Ltd; Peter Stothart, Wavefront Technologies; Christine Taylor, The Printed Picture Co; Prof. Nadia M. and Daniel Thalmann, Swiss Federal Institute of Technology; Tomato; Jane Unsworth, TDS Digitizers; Jim Valentine; Rudy VanderLans, *Emigré*; Alan Villaweaver, Cheltenham & Gloucester College of Higher Education; Mike Vince, Spark Sales Promotion; WHD; W Industries Ltd; Dr Keith Waters; Why Not Associates; Wickens Tutt Southgate; Matthew Wiessler, BBC Television; Ian Willis, Courtaulds Fabric Prints; Dominique Willoughby; Adam Woolfitt; Jacqueline Anne Wrather, Bournemouth Polytechnic; Brian and Geoff Wyvill; YRM Partnership Ltd; Peter Zenger, Computer Aided Architectural Visuals.

Additional picture credits

Contents

The Author

Professor John Vince is a research consultant at Rediffusion Simulation, where he advises on research activities into real-time 3D computer graphics. He was previously a Principal Lecturer at Middlesex Polytechnic, where he established the Computer Graphics Department. He has been associated with computer graphics for almost 20 years and his research activities have been in the area of applied computer graphics to art and design.

Professor Vince has recently been appointed Visiting Professor in Computer Graphics at Brighton Polytechnic and is also Chairman of the National Centre for Computer Animation at Bournemouth Polytechnic.

He is the author of three other books: *The Dictionary of Computer Graphics* (1984); *Computer Graphics for Graphic Designers* (1986); and *The Language of Computer Graphics* (1990).

Preface

A decade ago computer graphics was still evolving and although it was being used within CAD systems for architectural and engineering applications, very few artists and designers were able to enjoy similar benefits. Nowadays, anyone can purchase a powerful desktop system from their local computer shop. But the availability of hardware is only part of the story; there is also a tremendous wealth of complementary software for applications such as word-processing, desktop publishing, painting, typeface design, graphic design and 3D animation.

Although I would find it hard to believe that there could be artists and designers who have not heard of computer graphics, I could easily understand that they might not be aware of how advanced the subject has become. While researching this book, I too was surprised at the advances that have been made in recent years, and the number of young designers I met who saw their future working with computers.

This book reveals how computers are being used by different parts of the design industry, in particular the disciplines of graphic design, type and print, television graphics, architecture, fashion and textiles, animation and fine art. Chapter 1 explores the benefits digital techniques offer the designer, and also introduces the principles of computer graphics. The following chapters describe how computers are being used in the various disciplines with many illustrations to demonstrate how successful this has been. The final chapter looks to the near future and anticipates possible developments.

Because of the rapid rate of growth in hardware and software I decided not to identify too many products, because their life-span cannot be predicted, so the book does not offer advice on the kind of equipment to buy. Moreover, the aim of the book is to demonstrate that designers and computers have at last embraced one another, and we can look forward to a successful partnership between creative design and digital technology.

John Vince
June 1992.

'Life without industry is guilt,
and industry without art is brutality.'

JOHN RUSKIN

1 Introduction

COMPUTERS IN DESIGN

Approximately 50 years ago cumbersome electronic units were being assembled to form embryonic computers. Their inventors were planning to construct an electrical calculating machine capable of automating the repetitive and tedious arithmetic operations frequently encountered in the world of science and mathematics. Little did they realize that these were not the only areas in which their machines would be applied, for in the past two decades the technology of integrated circuits has launched our civilization into a technological revolution that knows no boundaries.

Nowadays, the refined digital computer has found its way into every facet of twentieth-century life, and the most surprising application of all has been in the world of design. Computers are being used by architects, interior designers, typographers, graphic designers, fashion designers, animators and fine artists. Computers are employed to design new typefaces, prepare advertising artwork, create synthetic images, visualize garments, retouch photographs, and even produce animations of objects that have no real existence.

The computer has become such an essential part of our working lives that we no longer question what it is, but enquire as to how it can be used to provide effective alternatives to existing working methods. Just as the telephone transformed international communication, so computers have revolutionized the way businesses function, with their talent for manipulating and storing data and translating it into useful information.

Computers are no longer seen as a threat. On the contrary, they enhance our mode of working, they make us more efficient, they relieve us of mundane tasks that they can perform effortlessly, and they have given us a creative freedom never before experienced with technology. Computer technology is so flexible that we can design systems to cater for any specific application. Indeed, it is so flexible that the same computer can assist a secretary in preparing a high-quality technical report, design a new typeface, paint a full-colour picture, draw a perspective view of a building, and even check the spelling and comment on the grammar of a manuscript.

Such dexterity is made possible by the software programs that ultimately drive a computer, and the fact that these are sold world-wide means that their unit cost is low and represents incredible value for money. For example, desktop publishing systems are available that incorporate most of the collective experience and knowledge accumulated over the past 500 years in the printing industry. Such systems provide access to a rich choice of fonts of various sizes, the ability to select bold, italic and headline styles, powerful features of justification, kerning and pagination, the integration of graphics, the automatic generation of indexes, the ability to preview pages on a display screen, and a multitude of other features. The computer's flexibility has meant that much more expert assistance has been made accessible to printers, publishers, authors, journalists and other professionals, as well as academics, students, and the lay public.

2

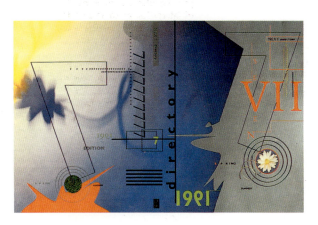

Computers have been a positive and radical stimulus in the way the written word is captured, manipulated and distributed, and they have provided a fantastic medium for the world of images. We are no longer obliged to use paper, canvas, or film to store an image: the digital domain of computer graphics provides a unique method of storing monochrome drawings, full-colour images, and detailed annotated line drawings, while also having the ability to create images electronically.

Prior to the computer, most images were stored as marks on paper — using materials like pencils, crayons, paint or ink — or held photographically. However, the computer complements these techniques with the virtual medium of digital signals, and all the benefits therein. Conventionally, a computer stores items such as a person's name, a date, or a temperature using a simple binary code which lends itself to all types of electronic manipulation and transmission. The same codes can also be used for describing images if they are reduced to a regular matrix of dots.

Turning pictures into patterns of dots is not a new concept: the printing industry has been using the halftone process for decades, but storing these individual intensities or colours as numbers has only been made possible by computer technology. To be effective, any picture must be represented by a large number of dots; perhaps millions, or thousands of millions of dots, which in turn can be manipulated by a computer. As modern computers are extremely fast, they can manipulate the most complex images with amazing speed.

What appears as a colour image on a computer screen is actually held within the computer's memory as billions of digital codes. This may seem to be awesome levels of data to manipulate, simply because we are not used to handling such large data sets, but to a computer it is second nature. The raw speed and reliability of modern computers means that they can digest data in seconds and create something totally new. For example, with the use of image processing techniques — initially developed for enhancing satellite images — a colour image can be scanned into a computer and enhanced to increase its sharpness. Colour and contrast balance can be modified and individual pixels (picture dots) can be altered. Pieces of the image can even be removed and replaced by another image. In fact, there are very few tasks that cannot be undertaken by a computer.

The paint system

One of the first computer-based systems to evolve in the world of computer graphics was the electronic paint system. This originated in the 1970s as a slow and expensive device, but showed so much potential that it was quickly developed into a specialist design aid which has transformed virtually every aspect of graphic design. Although the system still relies upon turning images into a matrix of pixels, it does not demand any input of original artwork. Instead, it allows the user to select a colour from a palette displayed upon the screen, and then using a particular style of painting or drawing (water colour, oil, crayon or chalk) begin sketching by moving a stylus over an electronic surface. The user's hand movements are then translated into marks of colour on the display screen — another creative demonstration of how effective the computer is in manipulating numbers.

Paint systems have had a profound impact upon graphic design by revealing unprecedented approaches to drawing. At no stage has the designer been deskilled: accurate and creative skills are still needed to originate any electronic image. However,

Quantel's Graphic Paintbox has revolutionized design studios throughout the world with its friendly user interface. A cordless, pressure-sensitive pen provides a natural mode of interaction to communicate painting styles, graphic effects, stencils, cutouts, type, and library searching.

The high-resolution screen (1,920 x 1,035) is used to view the contents of a 24-bit deep-frame store which is capable of holding images to a resolution of 5,440 x 3,712. The Quilt option permits a resolution of 14,000 by 14,000. *Courtesy: Quantel Ltd.*

Although paint systems were initially intended to support the video and television markets, it was quickly realized that their potential for visualization could be exploited in any design field.
   These three images by Hans Jorn Bøtcher demonstrate how an outline sketch can be rapidly translated into realistic renderings using Quantel's Video Paintbox.
Courtesy: PIXELS Aps, Creative Video Paintbox Studio.

an environment has been created uninhibited by the constraints of traditional techniques. Paint previously applied can be removed to leave a pristine canvas. Areas of the image can be enlarged to facilitate the drawing of fine detail. An online library can supply a vast source of images from which features can be extracted and input into the current image. The system's stylus can operate as a pencil, paintbrush, crayon or airbrush. Finally, in this incomplete list, two or more images can be composited using variable levels of transparency to create delicate effects that have become a creative hallmark of this technology.

   Although the above features are impressive, there is one more element that makes paint systems such a compelling technology — its ability to integrate images from different media. For example, photographs, paintings, drawings, video, satellite images and computer-generated images, can all be input to a computer, and once in a digital format can be combined as an integrated composite. Furthermore, the final image can be output photographically, printed on paper, recorded on video, broadcast on television, sent to another computer, or even sprayed on a gigantic canvas.

   Very early computer graphics systems were monochrome, and created pictures from collections of straight lines — hence the name vector graphics.

However, as computer memories became miniaturized and cheaper, the technique of raster graphics evolved, where individual pixel colours could be stored as numbers in a computer's memory. This technological development started the computer's journey along the road to rendering full-colour images, together with its important collaboration with video technology.

Television graphics

A colour television image is composed from a sequence of horizontal rasters, where on each raster the individual red, green and blue phosphor dots are activated by electron beams modulated by the video signal. This means that, given a block of memory called a frame store, a computer is able to store a video image as a matrix of pixel colour intensities. With the arrival of frame stores, it was a natural development to design software capable of manipulating these numbers and creating various graphic effects. Now this technology is very sophisticated: any video image can be manipulated as though it had a real geometric existence. It can be turned like a page, it can be folded into bizarre 3D objects, and it can be superimposed upon other video images to create a wealth of video effects.

It is understandable why computer-based systems have found their way into television; the industry, which employs the very latest in digital technology, would dearly miss its paint systems, digital video recorders, caption generators, and video effects machines. Television viewers would not be able to enjoy the high quality of design and creative flair that permeates modern television if the computer was not part of the design process. The world of advertising would also suffer if graphic designers were completely constrained by the limitations of traditional materials. The advertising industry

Designer Paul Butler created this image entirely on Quantel's Paintbox, after taking in the self-portrait of Edvard Munch via a rostrum camera. The photograph was colour mapped, and the x-and y-axes were distorted. A wash was also applied. The background map was also taken in via the rostrum camera, colour mapped and distorted. The photograph was then pasted over the map with a shadow.

The plane was drawn entirely on the Paintbox, 'cut out' and pasted over the other two images. The whole picture is a simple but effective build up of layers, all computer generated and manipulated. *Courtesy: Paul Butler.*

This synthetic image was rendered by a computer from numerical descriptions of 3D objects and 2D textures describing the scene. The renderer program uses optical laws describing the behaviour of light reflecting from surfaces, refraction through glass, and the creation of shadows. It also introduces texture for the carpet, wallpaper, television picture and the picture hanging on the wall to create an extra level of realism. The 6,000-line resolution image is taken from a 30-second animated commercial created for NOB Holland.
Courtesy: Buf/Duran and Softimage Ltd.

6

© Buf/Duran

employs some of the most sophisticated graphical applications of computers — 3D animation.

3D worlds

The cartoon animator is familiar with the labour-intensive methods of producing traditional cel-based cartoons. Every second of the final animation requires 24 separate images, which in turn may contain several cels. Each cel is hand-drawn and back-painted, making the entire process expensive and time-consuming. However, computer graphics has provided an alternative approach for creating the images. A 'virtual' 3D space is created in software where almost anything can be built, from a teapot to an entire planet. Once more, numbers are used to express the objects in a form easily digested by the computer. From these abstract blueprints further software reconstructs a photo-realistic image as seen by an imaginary camera. By changing the position of the camera (which is nothing more than a handful of numbers) or moving the objects, a different image is created. Furthermore, by instructing the computer to repeat this process over a defined time, an animated sequence can be output to film or video.

The state of this art is very advanced, and like paint systems has had a profound effect on all types of computer-generated imagery. In fact, the world of computer animation is leading us towards even more creative applications for computers. A world where we will be able to build, see and touch objects and images that have no real existence. A world where we can join our synthetic artefacts and interact with them in a way that is still difficult to comprehend.

Fashion

Visualizing something that does not yet exist is vital to the fashion industry, for they must anticipate what will sell next year, and what colour schemes will be

Special techniques are required to create the 3D surfaces of irregular objects, and in this example the animator used a photographic procedure. First, a plaster-cast sculpture was covered with a mesh of small polygons. Two photographs were then taken – one from the front and the other from the side. Using a conventional digitizer the photographs were digitized and it was possible to compute the x-, y- and z-coordinates for one half of the head. The coordinate data for the second half was then obtained by reflecting the original set.
Courtesy: Keith Waters.

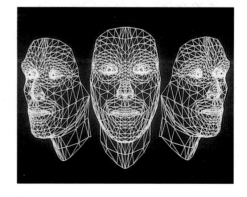

Design work by 3rd-year BA Knitwear Design student Debbie Abrahams. The project was carried out by students at Nottingham Polytechnic in conjunction with G Force of Nottingham and their knitwear design consultant, Gail Sallis. The students used CAD/CAM to generate portfolio illustrations, specification sheets and the finished product.
Courtesy: Brenda Sparkes, Nottingham Polytechnic.

acceptable to their clients. Preparing such artwork is time-consuming, especially when it comes to designing alternative combinations of colour, patterns and textures. However, introduce an electronic paint system into the design process and these problems are considerably simplified.

Once more, the computer's infinite flexibility scores over traditional methods, for it allows designs to be input and coloured using any palette of fashionable hues. By scanning in existing patterns, or even creating them electronically, a mannequin's garment can be displayed in various materials, to provide instant combinations. These pseudo three-dimensional views provide accurate information upon which commercial decisions can be made; much of the guesswork involved in the fashion industry has disappeared simply by using a computer.

Architecture

The ability to create imaginary three-dimensional worlds was quickly exploited by architects who discovered that computers could be used for visualizing proposals for new buildings. By feeding into a Computer Aided Design (CAD) system the dimensions of buildings, their relative positions to one another, existing highways and other topographical data, the computer can supply an infinite number of perspective views depicting the layout from ground-based and aerial views. Even animated walk-throughs can be produced, revealing visual detail to an accuracy that has no equal.

Although accurate visuals are very important in selling an idea to a client, the modern architect also depends upon computers for maintaining the vast number of annotated line drawings depicting exterior elevations, plans, floor layouts, cross-sections, and service routing. Paper-based drawings still play a vital role in providing a discussion document where modifications and extensions are made, but when such changes are finally implemented, the digital image is retrieved from the computer, corrected using high-resolution graphics screens, output to a laser plotter, and filed away on large magnetic disks. In this age of technological advances, paper is too delicate for storing such important information; its fragile qualities are no match for the robust, compact, flexible and accurate medium of digital signals.

Early CAD systems were expensive and only very large architectural practices could benefit from their utilization. However, with the dramatic increase in computer performance over recent years, together with the emergence of cost-effective PCs, computers have become a vital feature of the drawing office. Portable lap-tops, PCs, workstations and mini-

computers aid the architect's daily activities for preparing promotional literature, technical reports and feasibility studies, client presentations, conceptual designs, production information and general office management. The computer has become a catalyst for so many diverse activities that it is impossible to contemplate how the architectural profession would survive without them.

Creative benefits

So far in this introductory exploration of how computer graphics are being used in design applications, we have only explored the commercial applications and the creative benefits they bring to a variety of disciplines. But ever since the early days of computer graphics when computers were large and slow, and only equipped with rudimentary line drawing plotters, many fine artists recognized the emergence of a powerful medium through which they could develop new channels of expression. The computer's precision at placing marks on paper was unparalleled, and opened up totally new techniques for creating images. For example, although typewriters have been used for forming pictures from typographical symbols, the computer could not only translate photographs into a matrix of symbols, but the symbol itself could also be an image, making possible images of intense complexity. Such early explorative work clearly identified the accurate drafting skills that computers gave to the artist.

Another abstract feature that computers can offer the artist is randomness; computer programs can be written without being able to predict the outcome. This means that an artist can hide any mechanistic 'fingerprints' left by a computer program by introducing a degree of randomness. Any line drawn by the computer can be transformed from a perfect straight edge into a meandering curve, creating the

Don Miller, an art teacher at the University of Wisconsin, River Falls (USA), uses an Amiga 1000 microcomputer, a high-resolution monitor and a monochrome video camera in his image making. He considers the computer a flexible means of compositing his images:
   'The computer is the most logical and direct tool to aid the processing and realization of my ideas.'
   Above: A detail from Don Miller's *Chindi # 3*.
   Courtesy: Don Miller.

effect of a hand-sketched line. Colours can be disturbed from their consistent hues into textured patterns that suggest a human influence. Shapes can be distorted from their precise internally stored form into bizarre collections of related forms that suggest some degree of human intervention. In fact, a disturbing feature of computer systems is that they can be programmed with logic that suggests that some higher level of cognitive process is operating, where in reality it is nothing more than a pseudo-random process.

Clearly, computers have already made their mark. They have demonstrated that they are not just raw calculating machines, but when driven by intelligent software, can offer designers a stimulating and creative environment within which they can develop their images. Perhaps the major quality of computers is that they do not just replace some existing manual activity, but offer new ways of working with images that demand a totally new approach to image creation and manipulation. Visual effects that had pushed previous techniques to their limit suddenly become easily possible as technology advances.

There are many advantages in the virtual world offered by computers: paint and ink need no time to dry; images can be cut and pasted with soft-edged scissors and without glue; colour balance can be corrected with infinite precision; photographs, paintings, drawings and television pictures can be composited with computer-generated images; images can be stored on compact disks and sent anywhere in the world; and the highest quality artwork can be output onto any medium.

Computers have created a second Renaissance by stimulating every facet of creative design into exploring new avenues of image making, pushing back the frontiers of typography and print, revealing original methods for visualizing design concepts, and providing a three-dimensional world for viewing virtual structures.

THE COMPUTER

The modern computer did not just suddenly appear: its development can be traced back over several centuries in the form of mechanical aids to help mathematicians solve problems such as finding the square-root of a number to several decimal places. However, we have finally arrived at an electronic solution that appears to solve most of a mathematician's problems, as well as those encountered in art and design.

A simple, yet accurate description of a computer can be made by the following explanation. Consider a modern electronic calculator: this can undertake a wide range of arithmetic work when we type in the necessary operations. The answers are output upon liquid-crystal displays almost instantly because the calculator employs VLSI (Very Large Scale Integrated) circuits containing thousands of transistors. These are used to form special circuits that manipulate small pulses of electricity at a rate of billions per second. The pulses of electricity are called 'bits' and are used to represent the numbers inside the calculator. They are very convenient for the calculator's circuits, but rather cumbersome to use.

A computer contains similar circuits that undertake its arithmetic work just like a calculator; but in order to keep it operating at maximum speed, each operation is typed in advance into a memory unit. The more memory the computer has the more instructions can be held, which also implies that larger problems can be solved. The instructions that control a computer are called a program, which collectively are known as software.

Although the computer's circuits will rarely make a

Artist Kenneth Snelson's passion for finding visual interpretations of scientific and mathematical concepts is a thematic thread joining his stainless steel sculptures of 1968 to his computer-generated images of 1990. *Chain Bridge Bodies* (above) explores the powerful binding forces that are central to the stability of atomic structures. *Courtesy: Kenneth Snelson.*

mistake, it is quite likely that programs contain all sorts of errors and inconsistencies as they have been written by human programmers. However, modern programmers rely upon some very powerful software tools that minimize the introduction of errors, which is rather fortunate, as today's programs are becoming very large and sophisticated.

A modern Personal Computer (PC) is equipped with a Central Processing Unit (CPU), which contains the arithmetic unit and the main memory, a keyboard, a display screen, and a disk unit for storing software. It is also supplied with an important piece of software called the operating system, which makes the computer easy to use. We can then purchase application software, which is supplied on small disks to aid activities such as word-processing, database organization, sales forecasting, cost analysis and a host of others.

Some of these software packages contain hundreds of thousands of instructions, and consequently require large computer memories. The size of computer memories is always expressed in units of 'bytes', which represent eight of the digital bits processed by the electronic circuits. One byte is capable of storing one of 256 different codes, which enables it to store a letter from the alphabet, such as 'p' or 'R', a single digit, or even a punctuation mark. Although early computers only contained several thousand bytes, a modern PC may be equipped with several million bytes of memory. The term 'Kilo byte' or 'Kb' means approximately one thousand bytes (or more accurately 1,024 bytes), whilst 'Mega byte' ('Mbyte' or 'Mb') means approximately one million bytes (actually 1,024 x 1,024 bytes). With such large programs in use the disk units often have capacities measured in tens of Mbytes; some disk units even extend to thousands of Mbytes, known as a 'Giga byte' ('Gbyte' or 'Gb').

Every year, new circuits are released that push the computer's performance to higher and higher speeds. Currently, small PCs are capable of executing several million instructions per second (MIPS), with larger computers having a capacity of ten to a hundred times this figure. Specialist computer graphics systems exceed 1,000 MIPS. Why such a speed is needed cannot be appreciated until we have discovered how computers store images. However, before examining the world of computer graphics it is necessary to take a closer look at how the latest computers have been made so user-friendly.

THE FRIENDLY MOUSE

Issuing commands to a computer through a keyboard is not particularly efficient; not everyone can type quickly, and neither can they type without making mistakes. In recognition of this human failing, operating systems exist that allow commands to be made by pointing at screen icons or lists of instructions in the form of a menu. This provides the user with a clear range of alternatives without having to memorize lists of mnemonic codes.

The user points to the required icon or menu using a small hand-held plastic device called a mouse. When this is brushed against a desk-top or a special rubber mouse-mat, an internal ball rotates; this motion is translated into computer signals encoding the mouse's horizontal and vertical movements. The screen's cursor is then positioned by the signals from the mouse. The shape of the cursor varies depending upon the application software: for manipulating text, a vertical line is useful for inserting between letters, whereas for system commands an arrow shape may be used. When the cursor is suitably positioned, the user confirms a choice by operating a button on the mouse. This mode of

12

communication has become very successful as it has been implemented across a wide range of software, making it a relatively simple operation to master several different software packages.

Another important feature allows the user to look at two or more things simultaneously on a computer using the concept of a screen window. This is a rectangular area of the screen within which the user undertakes some task. However, if another window is 'opened', a new task can be commenced, and simply by moving the screen's cursor to the relevant window the user can move from one activity to another.

Collectively, the use of Windows, Icons, Menus and Pointers provides a WIMP interface and has been the breakthrough in computer interface design that has made computers so useful in design-based applications. This style of user interface was pioneered by Apple Computers and is responsible for the success of their Macintosh range of computers. Armed with this knowledge of computer technology we can now explore how these numerical machines can be incorporated into the design world.

The modern Personal Computer has at last provided individual users with extraordinary processing performance frequently exceeding several MIPS. The desktop system only requires a connection to an electrical supply and it is ready to work. Introduce an extra cable in the form of a Local Area Network (LAN) and it can communicate with computers on the same network.

Connect the system to a telecommunications network, and with the aid of fibre-optic cables and satellites the user can communicate with other computers around the world, where files of text and images can be transmitted and received at the speed of light. *Courtesy: Imagination Ltd.*

COMPUTER GRAPHICS

A close look at any computer terminal or television screen will reveal that they are covered in a matrix of light points called pixels. Some computer screens are monochrome, but a television screen is formed from red, green and blue phosphor dots to create full-colour images. To begin with, let us ignore the issues of colour and concentrate on the matrix of pixels and see how they can be used graphically.

Most computer graphics terminals operate like a television by sweeping a beam of electrons across the phosphor-coated screen of a cathode ray tube. The beam starts at the top left-hand corner, moves in a straight line towards the right-hand side and then returns back to the left-hand side with the beam suppressed ready for the next sweep one raster line down. In a television the odd lines are drawn in the first pass over the screen, followed by the even lines. This is known as interlacing, and is an effective method of creating more images without transmitting extra information. The increased refresh rate also reduces flicker. In computer graphics there is no need to broadcast the picture, therefore every raster can be accessed in one sweep to form a non-interlaced image. The rate at which the images are painted is called the refresh rate and is in the order of 60 images/second (60Hz; Hz is an abbreviation for Hertz who was a scientist associated with experiments with radio waves), which prevents the eye from detecting any flicker.

If the computer graphics terminal contains a block of memory whose contents are used to modulate the brightness of the electron beam during its journey across the phosphor, then a binary '1' in the memory would be interpreted as a bright spot, while a binary '0' would create a dark spot. So by ensuring that this memory contains the correct pattern of binary codes, an image can be created upon the screen.

If all of the memory stores binary '0', the screen will be dark, and if the memory only contains binary '1', the screen will be completely illuminated. There are no intermediate greys. So one of the tasks of computer graphics is to decide how this memory can be filled by the computer with binary patterns that form recognizable images. This form of image making is called bitmapping, due to the one-to-one correspondence between memory bits and screen pixels. The computer can send a binary '1' or '0' to any one of the memory locations by referencing its row and column numbers, and simple programs exist that enable a straight line to be drawn between any pair of screen pixels.

Storing line drawings

Although this method of line drawing is central to computer graphics display hardware, it cannot be used as the basis for maintaining all drawings within the computer. This is because the resolution of the screen, which is approximately 1,000 pixels by 1,000 pixels is insufficient to hold any detailed artwork. Nevertheless, the idea is sound and simply requires further development.

Instead of using actual pixel positions to fix the ends of our lines, an imaginary 2D space is used where any resolution is possible. This space is also free from an absolute system of units such as imperial or metric, although any one can be used when needed. This space also contains a reference point called the 'origin', from which all other points are located. For example, [2.45, 3.69] identifies a point which, by convention, implies it is horizontally 2.45 units to the right of the origin, and vertically 3.69 units above the origin.

Points to the left and below the origin are negative, thus a continuum exists for positioning any point relative to this origin. Furthermore, the horizontal and vertical offsets of the point are called its x- and y-coordinates respectively which are always used in this sequence for identifying it. Reversing them arbitrarily would lead to all sorts of confusion. Finally, diagrams showing points with x- and y-coordinates always have the x- and y-axes labelled to remind us of the correct convention.

This simple idea is central to all computer graphics as it provides a mechanism for storing many types of 2D artwork. For example, the letter 'H' can be stored by 13 points as shown on page 16; the table of coordinates indicates the precise journey taken around the letter, which in this case starts at the origin and proceeds clockwise. The starting point could have been any point, and the journey made anti-clockwise. In fact, the letter could have been placed anywhere relative to the origin. The memory required to store this letterform is not great: four bytes are needed for each coordinate, and as there

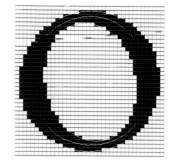

The digital nature of a computer's memory enables shapes to be stored as collections of bits. In this example, a bitmap of a 12pt letter O is shown enlarged. If it had been encoded within a matrix of 40 x 40 bits, 25 bytes of memory would be needed to store the bitmap. *Courtesy: The Electric Font Foundry Ltd.*

Computer graphics systems must be capable of storing a wide variety of designs, and one notation that is universally employed is that of Cartesian coordinates, where the position of any point on a plane is described with respect to a fixed origin. In this example, the point P is horizontally displaced from the origin 2.45 units, and vertically displaced 3.69 units – consequently, its coordinates are [2.45, 3.69]. Points to the left or below the origin have a negative sign to distinguish them from their positive counterparts.

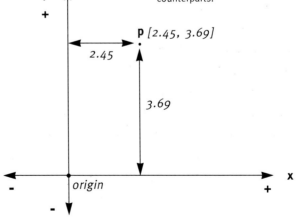

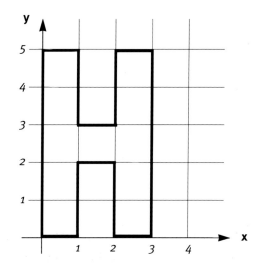

This letter H could be represented by a bitmap or an outline description using Cartesian coordinates. With the latter technique the end points of the edges must be defined in a clockwise or counter-clockwise sequence. In this example, the shape begins at the origin, proceeds clockwise and finally returns to the origin. If the starting and finishing points are both included, 13 pairs of coordinates are needed as shown in the table.

x	y
0	0
0	5
1	5
1	3
2	3
2	5
3	5
3	0
2	0
2	2
1	2
1	0
0	0

are 26 in all (2 x 13), a total of 104 bytes are consumed. It is important to remember that modern computers have memory sizes measured in Mbytes and disk storage measured in Gbytes.

Complex designs simply require more coordinates, consume extra memory and take more time to create. But storing smooth curves, especially font designs for a desktop publishing system, must not reveal any tell-tale jagged computer fingerprints, and this will require special attention. However, a wide range of applications can exploit this digitized form of artwork.

Digitizers can be used to create these files of coordinates, and they vary in size from A3 to A0 with an accuracy of at least 0.005 inch. The operator fixes to its surface the drawing to be digitized, and with the assistance of a stylus touches points on the contours. Care must be taken to digitize the boundaries in a logical sequence, and break points must be introduced between two contours.

Manipulating the image

The computer's ability to perform arithmetic operations such as add, subtract and multiply are all that is needed to scale and position any image stored within a computer. This means that if the coordinates of an A0 image could be digitized, then by multiplying them by 0.01 we could create another image the size of a postage stamp.

So far, we have not considered how to turn the numbers back into a drawing on paper, which is not a difficult operation. One of the earliest devices developed for computer graphics was the graph plotter, consisting of a pen which can be moved relative to a piece of paper. The plotter can be instructed to lift its pen up and down, and also move it in straight lines from one position to another using coordinate notation. If the plotter works in imperial units, then any coordinates sent to it will create a drawing equivalent to the scale determined by the magnitude of the numbers; a metric plotter would make a different conversion. Either way, the internal numbers can be converted into any system of units by introducing a suitable scaling factor.

If the plotter can hold Ao sheets of paper, our stored coordinates can be sent to it and the original image can be recovered, but if the coordinates are scaled by 0.01 and then plotted, a miniature drawing results. If the coordinates are scaled by 0.001, the plotter would still attempt to draw it, but it is highly likely that it would appear only as a spot of ink.

Coloured lines

The colour of the lines is obviously determined by the colour of the pen loaded in the plotter at the time of drawing, and most modern plotters are equipped with several pens of various colours which are automatically selected by a software package under the direction of the user. Filling in shapes with solid colour is difficult for a pen plotter, and the best that can be achieved is to employ programs that can create cross-hatching patterns. ('Cross-hatching' is a term used in technical drawing and describes the use of intersecting parallel lines to fill in an area or shape. A cross-section of an object is frequently 'cross-hatched'.) In overcoming this limitation, electrostatic plotters are available which transform the line information sent by the computer into a raster format. The image then appears from the plotter composed of very small dots, somewhat like a photocopying machine, with a typical resolution of 400 dots per inch (dpi).

Although early computer graphics systems produced their images upon paper using pen plotters, advances in bitmapped screens enabled line artwork to be viewed upon the user's display terminal. This requires a trivial program to convert the coordinate

values of the lines into screen pixels. Such a program ensures that the drawing can be displayed on all or part of the screen. Or at the other extreme, the display program can adjust its parameters such that only part of the drawing is seen on the whole screen; this effectively gives the user the ability to enlarge any portion of the drawing.

The principal features of a computer graphics system can be summarized as follows:

- A digitizer provides the means for the input of line artwork and its conversion into 2D coordinates.
- The computer provides a digital medium for storing this data and manipulating it.
- The display screen provides a temporary medium for viewing the internal representation of the numbers.
- A plotter captures the image on paper.

However, one of the main reasons for using computers with graphics is to exploit the interactive aspects of the technology, and programs must be written to achieve this.

Interactive programs

An interactive program will give us the ability to make alterations to the coordinate data. We may wish to move a point on a line to another position; an entire line may need deleting; an extra line might have to be introduced, or the entire image may need rotating through a small angle. Whatever the modification, the user must have an easy way of communicating these commands to the computer.

A conventional method of communication is for the interactive program to display a list of possible actions in the form of a menu on the screen. The user, with the aid of a mouse, places the screen's cursor over the required action and presses the button on the mouse twice to confirm the response. The pixel address of the cursor is read by the program and checked against its relative position in the menu. The computer then executes the instructions associated with the command and redraws the scene showing the modification. When the editing session is complete, the software package files the new data for a future session.

Even with computers working at 10 MIPS, very large data sets may cause delays when working interactively. Searching operations can take several seconds, and a few seconds may be needed to refresh the display screen. This is why faster computers are still required to satisfy the needs of some graphics applications.

The above brief description of an interactive system assumes that the images are displayed upon a monochrome bitmapped screen. This implies that the images could be shown black on a white background, or white on a black background. But if colour is needed, extra memory must be introduced for each pixel.

Coloured images

Early micro computers only had 16 colours (two of which were black and white), but with the advent of low-cost memory more colours could be used, and today it is usual to find personal computers capable of displaying 256 colours. More sophisticated systems can handle 16.7 million colours.

Coloured television pictures exploit the fact that the human visual system will register a colour sensation from different amounts of red, green and blue light. Thus when the red, green and blue phosphor dots are excited in a television set a continuous field of colour is experienced. This same principle is used in colour computer graphics, which means that extra memory is needed to store the red, green and blue components for each pixel. If each pixel is allocated three bytes — one for each primary colour — then the 8 bits making up each byte enable 256 levels of intensity to be held. This means that with 256 levels of red, green, and blue, a total of

16.7 million colour shades (256 x 256 x 256) are possible. For a screen with 1,024 x 1,024 pixels, 3Mb are required to hold the displayed image, which accounts for the computer's higher price.

Another alternative to full-colour systems is to use a memory store having one byte for each pixel which means that only 256 colours can be displayed, but these can be chosen from the 16.7 million and still offer a useful facility in many applications.

Most PCs only have the ability to display 16 colours, but can easily be modified to display a wide range of screen and colour resolutions simply by fitting a graphics card. This contains the extra memory needed to store the image. One popular format is VGA, which has a standard resolution of 640 x 480, but it can be extended to 1,024 x 768 and can display 256 colours from a palette of 256K. Other boards can provide a screen resolution of 1,280 x 1,024 with 16.7 million colours, and will also need a suitable high-resolution monitor.

Colour control

Given that colours are held in the computer as mixtures of red, green and blue, we still have the problem of interfacing artists and designers who do not think in these terms. Some users may wish to use the idea of levels of hue, saturation and lightness, whilst others may only be conversant with colour mixing using cyan, magenta and yellow. Fortunately, all of these colour models are related to one another, in that a colour specified in CMY (cyan, magenta and yellow) can be converted to RGB (red, green and blue) within the computer.

It is true that these relationships exist, but only for known specifications of red, green, blue, cyan, magenta and yellow. Furthermore, it is generally known that different televisions produce widely different colour characteristics. This is due to the way they have been adjusted and to the phosphors used in the cathode ray tube, which is why self-calibrating monitors (see Glossary) are very useful in resolving some of these issues.

Another important aspect of colour control is highlighted when a stored image is output to film or paper. An ink-jet printer will have different colour characteristics to a colour photocopier, which also vary from one manufacturer to another. Even the colour bias of film changes from one manufacturer to another, which makes the control of colour from input to output a delicate process. However, ways to maintain a firm control over colour consistency are discussed in later chapters.

No matter which system the user wishes to employ, an interface can be designed to allow a prefered colour space to be used, but internally, the computer's software is converting everything into levels of RGB, CMY or any other type of coding.

PAINT SYSTEMS

One obvious application in computers is for electronic painting. If the computer can hold the colour for each pixel, it could be left to the user to interactively control those pixels that should be painted. Nowadays, Quantel's Paintbox is the *de facto* standard for the broadcast industry as it was designed specifically for use in television, and incorporates unique hardware circuits to give true real-time interaction. Other paint systems are also available based upon personal computers which provide different facilities for other types of users.

Basically, a paint system converts the position of a stylus on a tablet (a small digitizer) into a screen's pixel address, and as the stylus is moved about in real-time, numbers are being 'sprayed' into the computer's memory to form the picture. This memory

Paul Anscombe's *Mother, Dear Mother* was painted on an IBM XT PC using the Imigit paint system. Even though its colour palette was restricted to 256 colours, these were exploited by the artist to develop a colourful and vital scene. *Courtesy: Paul Anscombe and Bournemouth and Poole College of Art and Design.*

is also being scanned at approximately 60 times a second (60Hz) to create the video signal.

The effective size of the brush represented by the stylus is also user-defined, starting from one pixel, up to a radius of several hundred pixels. But the thicker the brush becomes, the more pixels have to be updated, which means more work for the computer. And even with computers working at several MIPS, it is still difficult to always provide real-time interaction, hence the reason for dedicated hardware to perform this work. However, modern PCs are becoming extremely fast and with the right software can offer a cost-effective performance.

To speed up the application of electronic paint, the stylus can mimic brush sizes of any diameter with a hard or soft edge. A soft-edged brush is achieved by making the colour intense at the centre of the brush mark, with lower intensities at its periphery. With the right distribution, an airbrush effect is possible, which is useful for adding highlights or blending together different graphic elements. Speckle or spray effects are possible by having a random collection of points to represent the brush, and only the pixels addressed by these points are updated.

The final image can be stored on disk and retrieved at any time. The disk storage required for an image will depend upon image and colour resolution, but assuming that the image was approximately 1,024 by 1,024 pixels, each having three bytes for the red, green and blue components, 3Mb are needed to store it on disk. Further features of paint systems will be explored in later chapters where they are used for specific applications.

ALIASING

Computer-generated images suffer from various artefacts such as jagged edges which come under the heading of aliasing. On a screen capable of displaying either black or white, little can be done to alleviate aliasing without sacrificing other features of the image, but when a pixel can register a range of grey levels an edge can be softened by introducing extra pixels of different intensities. This is called anti-aliasing. Such techniques — and there are many — need to know the existing background colour and the proportion of the pixel covered by the line to determine its intermediate shade. This makes extra work for the computer and can slow it down.

A simple method of anti-aliasing is to compute the image to a higher resolution and derive a low-resolution version by averaging groups of pixels. As an example, one could compute an image to 1,024 by 1,024, and then find the average colour intensities for neighbouring groups of 2 by 2 pixel squares to create an image 512 by 512. Although this does not produce optimum results, it is quick and effective.

3D COMPUTER GRAPHICS

Defining points on a drawing or display screen using x- and y-coordinates seems a natural way of describing two-dimensional shapes. However, computers are not restricted to two dimensions, they are equally at home working with three dimensions if

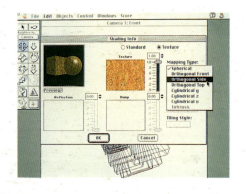

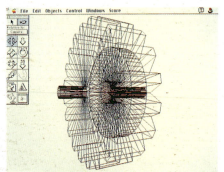

we are prepared to input the necessary 3D geometry. If we can supply a computer system with the x-, y- and z-coordinates describing an object, then with the aid of various computer graphics techniques, we can obtain perspective views of this data from any point in space. In fact, this imaginary space is often referred to as 'world space', and by defining the location of an imaginary observer and a focal point, there is sufficient 3D information for the computer to display what would be seen from this position.

The action taken by the computer is very similar to the way a perspective image can be captured upon a sheet of glass; so imagine standing in front of a window through which some outside scene is viewed. Then assuming that one can reach the window with an outstretched arm, it would be possible to trace upon the glass using a marker pen features of distant 3D objects. Near objects would probably have a large projected image on the window, while distant ones would be small. This action captures upon the glass a perspective projection of the outside 3D scene.

This same perspective projection can be simulated within the mathematical world space of a computer program. All that is required is a collection of 3D coordinates describing some imaginary group of objects, together with the position and orientation of an observer who is gazing through a mathematical sheet of glass. Although this last requirement sounds strange, it can be achieved with school geometry.

3D computer graphics systems are thus able to prepare perspective views of any set of 3D coordinates. The computer projections would normally appear as a collection of lines obeying the standard laws of perspective, and could appear very confused unless extra software is used to hide those lines that would be obscured by other features of a scene. For example, if a 3D computer system was used by an architect to design a new building, some

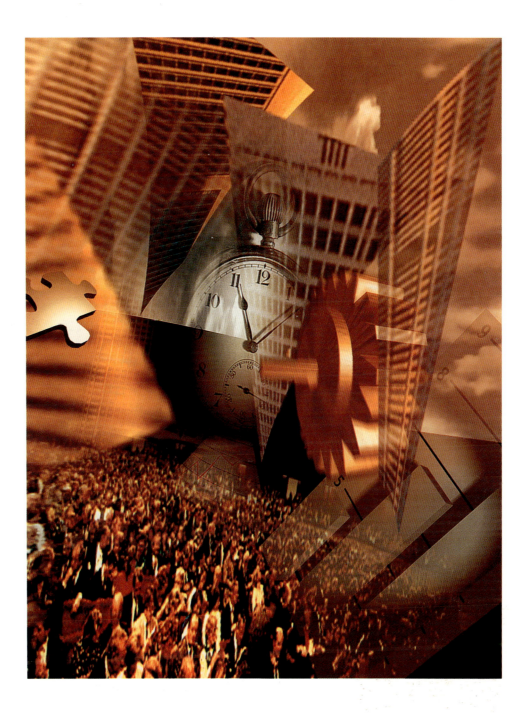

Above: Cover designed by
Peter Crowther for a Leisure
Management Group brochure.
Simple models of the bar
chart, cog and jigsaw piece
were created in Swivel 3D and
the images were montaged
together in Photoshop.

Left: Images showing how the
cog was developed on screen
(top and middle) and the
finished model (bottom).
Courtesy: Peter Crowther.

parts of the structure will hide other features, and such spatial conflicts must be resolved by hidden-line removal programs. When the data sets become very large, which often happens in practice, even large computers require many minutes or hours to resolve these problems.

The final perspective image need not be shown in line form, for sophisticated rendering programs exist for computing the colour intensities at each pixel. However, as there are normally more than one million pixels on a screen, this task can also present a massive computational problem for some computers.

Designers can obtain many benefits from such techniques; all they require is an interactive system for creating the 3D database and the complementary software to provide different views.

HARD COPY

It is all very well creating coloured images inside a computer, but at some stage they need to be captured on paper or film. Both media are possible but one cannot expect the colour gamut of the monitor to match that of film or a paper printing process. The light emitted by a monitor has a luminous source, while a printed image is seen with reflected light, and these two processes alone introduce subtle differences in the perception of colour. Furthermore, different films have a bias towards certain parts of the spectrum, which implies that if any degree of consistency is to be introduced into image capture, one must develop a thorough working knowledge with these media characteristics.

An image can be captured on film in various formats and resolutions, but one process involves sending the three colour separations to a high-quality flat monochrome screen which is photographed through three primary colour filters. For example, the red component is displayed as white light and photographed through a red filter, followed by the green and blue components with their corresponding filters. Another process involves a film being exposed to a small beam of light which passes through three primary colour filters.

An image can be captured on paper using electrostatic plotters, ink-jet printers, laser plotters or thermal printers. Each leaves behind their own 'fingerprints' in the form of colour preferences and resolution, but the trend is definitely towards extremely high-quality colour reproduction.

Laser copiers
Laser copiers have always been seen as stand-alone devices, but their technology was quickly exploited

The digital nature of images stored inside a colour copier means that it can be subjected to a variety of image processing operations. Here we see two examples of how an original image can be squashed and stretched.

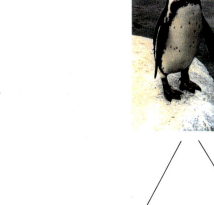

within laser plotters. Recently, colour laser copiers have appeared with interfaces that permit them to be driven by a computer. For example, the Canon CLC 500 colour copier possesses many features found on an electronic paint system. Original images can be viewed and manipulated, and their colour balance can be altered. But one of its most useful features is that digital colour files can be sent directly from a computer and output on paper in full colour.

We have had to wait a long time for this technology to arrive, and even though current systems are producing excellent images with 400 dpi, this is only the beginning of high-quality image output on paper and film. Some systems can already create halftone images that only betray their origins under magnification.

It is now possible to examine how the disciplines of graphic design, typography, television graphics, fashion design, architecture, animation and fine art employ computer graphics, and discover how computers have created a new world for design.

'That is the best part of beauty, which a picture cannot express.'

SIR FRANCIS BACON

2 Graphic Design

Above: CD cover designed by
John Warwicker and Graham
Wood at Tomato. The type and
design was created in Aldus
FreeHand. The cover also
includes photographic and
painted elements.
Courtesy: Tomato.

Left: Barclays Graduate
Recruitment Brochure 1992/3
cover. The images were
scanned in and transferred to
a Paintbox, for colour
correction and combining.
*See Acknowledgements page
for credits.*

DIGITAL PICTURES

Before exploring the uses of computers within graphic
design, perhaps it will be useful to define the scope
of this area of activity. Primarily, this chapter
addresses design activities like the graphic layout of
brochures, stationery, posters, books, magazines,
packaging, corporate identities, dust covers and
record sleeves; where the role of the graphic designer
is to select appropriate materials, devise original
logos, develop house styles, identify colour schemes,
select suitable typefaces, and even design
appropriate new letterforms.

A skilled graphic designer can, with the creative
use of colour, layout and type, capture a feeling of
quality, security, reliability, excitement, warmth,
respectability and even humour. Creative art and
design is also a powerful commercial force that
persuades us to buy food, books, holidays, and
records on the basis of the packaging as well as the
contents. The sensitive use of text, images, colour,
and paper can communicate subconscious messages
that written text alone could never convey. However,
successful designs do not just happen. Designers
require a fertile imagination, experience and the
tenacity to explore 'what if' scenarios – which is
where the computer comes in.

A decade ago graphic designers had little

These two enigmatic images, *Nadir* (above), and *Aspirations* (*9 A.M.*) (right), by Dominique Willoughby were created with a Quantel Graphic Paintbox. They contain graphic effects that would be difficult to realize in any other medium. *Nadir* was awarded first prize in the digital image category at Paris Cité 1991. *Courtesy: Dominique Willoughby.*

exposure to computer graphics. This was probably fortunate, as early systems were far from user-friendly, and required incredible tenacity to achieve the smallest level of assistance. But during the intervening years these embryonic systems have developed beyond all recognition, and nowadays the computer's digital technology can be applied to every aspect of image manipulation – from the use of lasers in colour copiers, to the creation of animated synthetic images.

Graphic designers have discovered a new design language in a world where there are no boundaries defining the end of one process and the start of another. A world where images can be integrated using the universal digital language of pixels to build seamless layers of colour.

There is now a real awareness that at last an integrated industry exists for the digital creation, manipulation, transmission and reproduction of high-quality images. The key to this integration has been digital technology which introduces a discrete coding system for storing picture elements. Video devices such as cameras, cassette recorders, video disk players and TV tuners are all capable of supplying a signal for digital encoding, and even the familiar 35mm camera has a digital equivalent capable of storing its images on a floppy disk.

The latest in laser colour copiers also exploits digital techniques which enable it to copy full-colour images with great precision, and it also behaves as a valuable computer peripheral. In an input mode, an image can be scanned – perhaps to a resolution of 400 dpi – and the pixel values input to a host computer. While in an output mode, any digital image can be sent to it and reproduced on paper.

Connect all of the above devices together as part of a computer system, and one has an amazing digital medium for image manipulation. Introduce a network of fax channels, modems and satellites, and the medium encompasses the world, where a full-colour image can be created on a computer in one country and become part of a magazine advertisement in another, without ever appearing on paper in an intermediate form.

This range of technology provides a wealth of sources from which designers can capture images. The still video camera can capture good-quality images on a floppy disk which, without any further processes, can be input to a page makeup system and composited with other artwork. A video camera's output can be input to a computer where it can be integrated with other sources of media, or stored on a compact disk which can then be read back in a random sequence. This technology is called CD-ROM (Compact Disk-Read Only Memory) and has allowed computers to be used in interactive multi-media applications, where images, sound and text are manipulated simultaneously.

Computer images can be captured upon monitors, laser printers, colour copiers, bromide, electrostatic plotters, transparencies, video tape, laser disk, magnetic tape, and laser projectors. They have interfaces to virtually every other form of technology, and are providing designers with a very flexible medium upon which they can place their marks. The

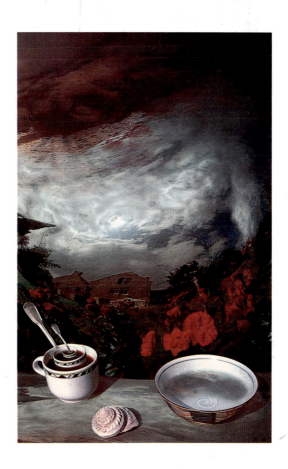

To create this Heineken poster, initial experimentation with textures was carried out on the Dash 3oFX using Painter software. The results were transferred to the Paintbox. A mask was created to isolate the tankard, through which the background was restored. The tankard was retouched and the edges broken up to integrate it with the background.
See Acknowledgements page for credits.

computer is a catalyst for integrating processes for image creation, manipulation and reproduction, and like any other medium requires understanding if its full potential is to be realized.

Many design studios employ a variety of computer-based design aids and require designers who understand and can exploit such systems, and although it goes without saying that the technology is dead without the creative input, it is also important to note that these systems possess latent features that even their inventors had not contemplated. For example, who would have imagined using a colour laser copier as a fine art medium? Who, too, could have appreciated that some of the image processing effects used in enhancing images for robots would have applications in paint programs? In order to appreciate the potential offered by computer-based systems one must examine some of the available systems and the features they offer.

RESOLUTION

Image resolution is not an issue with a traditional medium such as paint, although it is a feature of photographic film which has an inherent grain size. In general, the faster the film, the larger the grain size. But in practice, a photographer is able to choose from a wide range of film stock to create any desired effect, which may even emphasize the film's grain characteristics. In the digital world of images, however, resolution is a vital parameter.

A television image contains less than 500,000 picture elements, which although a large number, severely restricts the level of detail that can be realized on this medium. Consequently, an electronic paint system for the television industry need only store images to this resolution. But if the computer is to be used for processing photographs, the system resolution is vital to its effectiveness.

An image is converted into a digital form by image scanners which sample colour intensities at regular points over its surface. The process mimics the raster system used in television technology by scanning the image on a line-by-line basis, and for each line generates the three colour separations for every pixel. For example, a 35mm transparency scanner might have a resolution of 180 lines per millimetre, and would create approximately 20 million pixels. However, in a full-colour system, each pixel will require 3 bytes for encoding the three colour components, which means that 60Mb would be needed to store the digitized image.

Quantel's Graphic Paintbox XL system has in excess of 200Mb of image storage memory, as it is capable of working with images held to a resolution of 5,440 by 3,712 pixels. The 'Quilt' option extends the image resolution to 14,000 by 14,000, but only a window of 5,440 by 3,712 is sampled at any time for display purposes. Crosfield's Mamba paint system can also process high-resolution images but employs a mixture of RAM (Random Access Memory) and disk to provide the user with 4Gb of virtual memory. Such systems also provide the user with a short-term library for images in the form of disks which have capacities measured in hundreds of Gbytes, and

magnetic tape for long-term archiving.

Even though a large memory is capable of storing a high-resolution image, current display technology cannot provide a cost-effective monitor for viewing it. Therefore, the actual displayed image might only have a resolution of 1,920 by 1,035 pixels, as in the case of Quantel's system. This does not mean that the designer is unable to work with the complete image, for the internal version is sampled at the screen resolution to incorporate the colour contribution of surrounding picture elements.

This sampling process, together with the nature of monitor phosphors, can introduce an attractive softness to the image which does not restrict an operator from creating or manipulating the finest detail. However, once the image is output onto a colour transparency the crispness of the original image reappears.

Although computers are extremely fast, with speeds measured in tens of MIPS, when they have to update large image files containing Gbytes of data, they cannot be expected to provide an instantaneous response. Consequently, short delays, perhaps measured in minutes, must be expected whilst they undertake such tasks. No doubt these delays will disappear as more powerful, and therefore faster, processors become available.

This image was created
entirely from one transparency
using a Graphic Paintbox. The
benefits of electronic special
effects are clearly
demonstrated in this personal
project by Bruce Brouwn,
where anamorphic distortions,
glows, ghosting and blending
have been used to develop an
impossible image.

*Concept and image
manipulation: Bruce
Brouwn/Photolaboratories
Souverein BV, Weesp, Holland.
Photography: Bienete
Koedijk/Souverein Studios.*

32

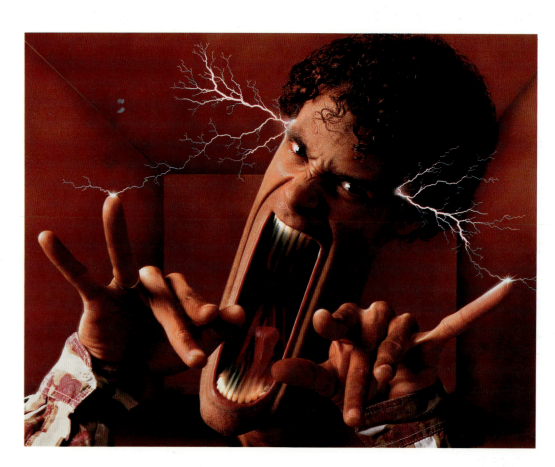

INPUT AND OUTPUT

Scanners are used for converting the original artwork into a digital form. This may be a transparency scanner or a flatbed scanner for artwork prepared on paper or a similar medium. It is also possible to capture an image from high-definition television (HDTV) cameras which are now capable of resolving 1,035 lines, each containing 1,920 pixels. Interfaces also exist in magnetic tape form from scanners employed in the print industry in formats such as Crosfield, DDES, DNS, Hell and Scitex, which means that modern high-resolution paint systems can work with virtually any type of technology.

As the internal image format is digital it means that it can be written to magnetic tape for input to other computerized printing systems. The digital nature also guarantees that it will arrive noise-free, will not degrade over time, and will introduce a quality and consistency unmatched by any other process. The digital signal can also be used to drive colour printers, and laser printers for immediate proofs or medium-resolution artwork. But the highest quality is realized when used to make a 10-inch by 8-inch colour transparency. A standard output resolution is 40 lines per millimetre.

It would be impossible to list and describe all of the features found on modern paint systems, but it is worth addressing some that are unique to this mode of image creation.

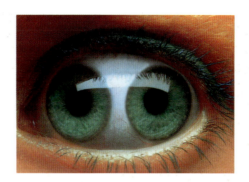

This image was prepared on Quantel's Graphic Paintbox, and clearly demonstrates the seamless continuity of image quality that is now possible with state-of-the-art technology. *Image manipulation: Photolaboratories Souverein BV, Weesp, Holland. Courtesy: Souverein-Koningsveld Studios.*

PAINTING MODES

Colours can be mixed on-screen and used to develop a palette associated with the current image, and they can also be used directly from the image to guarantee that any retouching is totally invisible. A portion of the image, or the entire image, may be treated with a wash of colour, made brighter or

These photographs of a Nissan Europe prepared on a Paintbox, provide valuable and accurate visualizations of the car's appeal in different colour schemes.
Image manipulation: Bruce Brouwn/Photolaboratories Souverein BV, Weesp, Holland. Photography: Peter Boudestein.

darker, or even made sharper through the use of image processing techniques.

The applied colour can behave like real paint – from the gentle application of a transparent watercolour, to the opaqueness of oils. Surface texture can be introduced through embossing effects, together with ghosting and luminescent glows.

Perhaps one of the strangest effects is that of 'un-painting', where the system is switched into a reverse mode and actually moves back in time, removing previously laid brush strokes to some earlier status. This means that the system must have been storing those parts of the image being updated, and as this needs internal RAM or disk memory, only a limited period of activity can be preserved.

The 'virtual brush' can be set to any radius – with or without a soft edge. It can even emulate the delicate distribution of colour intensity normally associated with traditional airbrushing. The shape of the brush stroke might be an arbitrary design selected from an image, which also means that several hundred colours will leave their individual imprint as the brush is moved.

Stencils

With traditional techniques, the introduction of a new element into an image was always let down by the quality of the edges. However, on electronic paint systems, soft-edged stencils enable any portion of an image to be replaced without any 'fingerprints'. This feature, which is vital to successful retouching processes, uses an extra overlay of memory covering the internal image. The memory is 1 byte deep and because of its ability to store 256 intensity levels, it can provide a mechanism for soft-edge feathering for the stencil. When this extra transparency information in the memory is combined with 24-bit colour files, a 32-bit file is created where the 8-bit overlay is called the alpha channel.

To isolate any portion of the image, the 'stencil mode' is selected to activate the stencil memory. The user now paints over the desired portion of the image, but instead of new colour going into the picture memory, the stencil store is filled and would appear on the screen as a coloured overlay. The display system blends together the contents of the image and stencil store to create a composite transparent image on the monitor.

If a soft-edge stencil is required, an airbrush mode is used to complete the border of the stencil, otherwise a hard edge is created which is also vital for certain types of work. The user can now remove that part of the image under the stencil and place it somewhere else on the image, or perhaps store it in

Realism is vital when assessing the design merits and visual impact a package will have on consumers. It frequently involves expensive mock-ups and photographic sessions, but now this can all take place within the virtual world of paint systems. In this example, a designer's sketch was quickly transformed into a photo-realistic image using Quantel's Video Paintbox. A video camera was used to input text and pictures of pieces of fruit, and then the Paintbox operator made the final transformation using stencils and airbrushing. *See Acknowledgements page for credits.*

a library for compositing with another image. If the stencil has a soft edge, its intensity is used to control the degree of colour removed, which ensures that when the stencil portion is recombined with another image the blend is invisible.

Stencils are used in myriad ways such as moving elements from one part of an image to another, changing the colour of selected portions of an image, removing unwanted features of an image, or resizing parts of an image.

Zoom, pan and rotate

It is possible to magnify any part of the image by repeatedly selecting a rectangular window which is then made full-screen size. It is unnecessary to allow the user to zoom into such a level that the entire screen contains one picture element, therefore most zoom operations stop when an internal image pixel is clearly seen as a square of colour. This means that any picture element from 20 million can be individually addressed and processed. Whilst in a zoom mode, the image can be panned in any direction so that any parts of the image which are off-screen can be examined.

An image can even be rotated through any angle, and extraordinary levels of computer processing power are needed to achieve a real-time response. You may recall from Chapter 1 that personal computers run at various speeds varying from one to several MIPS, depending on their architecture and processor. It is interesting to note that Quantel's Graphic Paintbox has an effective processing speed in excess of 1,000 MIPS. One thousand million instructions per second is impossible to comprehend, yet it is an interesting reminder that this degree of processing power is needed to simulate a task like rotation or scaling, which only requires a pair of hands using paper.

Typefaces

Most paint systems provide a variety of fonts which can be painted, airbrushed, scaled, rotated and distorted. Some even enable a group of words to be surrounded by a collection of control points, which when moved, pull or push the individual letters into new shapes. This is a very powerful and useful feature and saves hours of painstaking drafting time if undertaken manually.

The user interface

Paint systems come in a variety of disguises, from the most primitive (given away free with small micro computers) to the most sophisticated (employed in state-of-the-art design studios). However, between these two extremes there exists a wide variety of systems that have been designed to match the range of graphic needs of the design industry. A top-of-the-range system would not be employed to develop throw-away business graphics presentations; neither would a low-cost PC system be successful in retouching sophisticated high-resolution images.

In spite of the wide range of available systems, with totally different specifications, they tend to have a consistent user interface making it relatively easy to move from one system to another. Obviously no programming is involved as the system is driven by software written by the manufacturer. The operator simply activates the package on a PC, or just picks up the digitizing stylus on a professional system and begins painting. Commands are displayed in the form of menus on the screen and are executed by touching the relevant word or icon using a mouse or stylus. Very little keyboard activity is required as the WIMP environment creates a friendly level of interaction.

One of the confusing aspects of computer technology is the variation in cost over a group of apparently similar systems. For example, a paint system on a micro computer could be given away with the computer, but would have very little application in the professional design world. But the difference between a dedicated paint system and a low-end PC-based system could be a factor of 100:1. The reason for this difference in quality and application must be understood by any design practice contemplating purchasing a computer.

Such a wide range of systems exists to address the breadth of the market, and for certain products such as record and video sleeves it would be foolish to ignore the benefits of a low-cost PC-based paint system. Top-of-the-range PCs running modern full-colour software packages are a tempting choice for any graphic design studio. However, the dedicated paint systems for storing and processing ultra high-

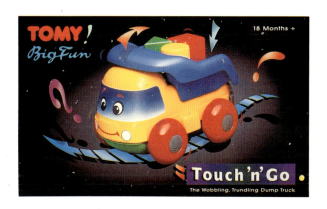

'Big Fun' is one of two radical new brand identities created by design consultants Wickens Tutt Southgate for toy manufacturer Tomy's Pan European pre-school range. The 'Big Fun' packs were designed using a Quantel Graphic Paintbox, with the help of computer graphics company Harmer Holbrook. Photographs of the product were scanned in and assembled with drawing and lighting effects; lighting, photography and illustration were all broken down digitally and reassembled to form a seamless whole.
Courtesy: 'Big Fun Touch n' Go' designed by Simon Coker of Wickens Tutt Southgate for Tomy.

In this collage of four transparencies, an inventive and amusing image has been created from a background texture, a pair of hands and an eye. Quantel's Graphic Paintbox was used to introduce the soft filtering effect on the background, modify the skin colour of the hands and paint the yellow and red markings. The turtle shell was then painted and enhanced with an embossed effect. Finally, the ensemble was composited to create an image of stunning quality that is now synonomous with digital technology.
Courtesy: Colour Club Brussels, Belgium.

resolution images are still necessary.

To illustrate this point further, consider the process of photomontage, this consists of three stages: the scanning in of several transparencies, their interactive composition, and the final output of colour separations. A typical project might involve 30 minutes for scanning, one hour for manipulation, and perhaps 15 minutes to output the colour separations. However, as technology advances, a scanning device may be invented which will digitize any image in a fraction of a second, and even output the result in the same time.

Applications

The expression 'the camera never lies' is almost true if one ignores the distortion and other artefacts introduced by a lens, but it cannot be applied to the photographs it takes. Once a photograph has been processed by an electronic paint system, visual untruths can be introduced to fool the most experienced photographic detective. Consequently, an obvious application for high-resolution paint systems is in photographic retouching. Conventional retouching of negatives is still a thriving commercial activity, and will probably remain so for some years to come; there are still many retouching operations that are quicker and cheaper to perform manually.

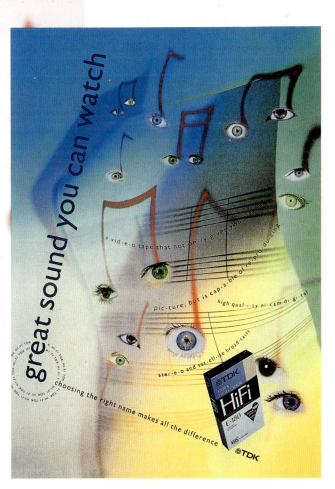

This TDK advertisement was designed by Siobhan Keaney and executed (with the help of Mark Bullen) on a Quantel Graphic Paintbox.

Photographs taken by Robert Shackleton were comped together graphically and the type on the manuscript paper was shot separately and then scanned into the system.

The transparencies, a pack shot of a TDK video cassette and a paper trace were comped together. The red paper notes and then the eyes were added and given highlights and shadows. Colour was later washed onto the irises.
Courtesy: Siobhan Keaney.

A series of brochure covers for
Nationwide Building Society.
Above left: Capital Bond
Direct. Above right:
FlexAccount. Right: Prestige
Bond Plus.
 The backgrounds were taken
from a transparency which was
colour-corrected and blended.
The type was distorted on a
Macintosh and transferred to a
Paintbox, coloured and given
an edge. The other elements
were taken from transparencies
and soft shadows were added
to give a 'floating' impression.
*See Acknowledgements page
for credits.*

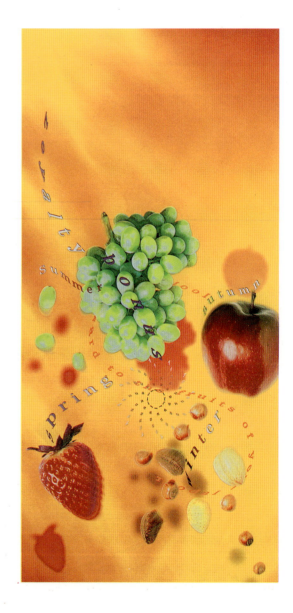

However, when it comes to many of the delicate and complex retouching methods associated with the preparation of modern artwork, the computer paint system has no rival.

Photomontage has taken on a new meaning with the introduction of high-resolution paint systems, for not only has the quality increased out of all proportion, but the technology is allowing for the first time, effects that were hitherto impossible. A designer's visual vocabulary has been significantly enhanced by this new medium, which although is supported by a sophisticated technology, is so transparent that virtually anything is possible. Electronic paint systems are being used for designing record sleeves, mail-order catalogues, photo retouching, advertising, posters, corporate brochures and product visualization. In fact, there are no restrictions; they can be used wherever high-quality images are needed.

PC systems

One of the most significant developments in recent years has been the impact PC systems have had on small design studios. In the past, many were unable to purchase the large and expensive computer-based design aids for obvious commercial reasons. However, there now exists an amazing wealth of

To create the final image for the National Power Annual Report 1991 cover (bottom) the branding and Wattage were removed from the surface of the lightbulb and the element was removed from within. The map was supplied as line artwork and scanned into the paintbox. Soft-edged masks were used to create a glow effect, before positioning it inside the lightbulb. *See Acknowledgements page for credits.*

THE TWENTY FIFTH OF MAY : GO WILD

25th of may

This digi pack CD was
designed by Simon Taylor and
Graham Wood at design group
Tomato. The type was created
in Aldus FreeHand and the
photography compiled from
four individual shots in
Photoshop.
Courtesy: Tomato.
Art direction: Simon Taylor.
Photography: David Sims.

hardware and software whose cost is a fraction of a typical designer's salary. The computer has rapidly become an essential design aid which quickly pays for its initial outlay, and then continues to be profitable thereafter. The Apple Macintosh range of computers has established an enviable position in this marketplace: such systems are easy to use, there is a wide range of application software to choose from, they operate in an office or studio environment, and they are affordable by small businesses.

One cannot underestimate the importance user-friendliness has played in the speed with which the design community has embraced computers. Designers generally have little or no interest in what happens beneath the plastic surface of a computer – they just want to switch it on and use it for some design task. Fortunately, today's computers are easy to use; most software packages are the system's personality, and the computer hardware is virtually transparent when in use.

Application packages such as Aldus FreeHand, PageMaker, Adobe Illustrator, and PixelPaint Professional are just some of the software packages being used every day by designers to create book covers, brochures, record sleeves, business stationery, menus, business cards, packaging, technical illustrations, and a thousand-and-one other

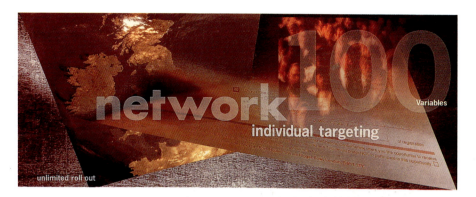

Above: 'The Lifestyle Network'
NDL cover, designed by Peter
Crowther for Mellor Design.
Scanned images were montaged
together in Photoshop, adding
depth and perspective. The
typography was also applied
within Photoshop.
Courtesy: Peter Crowther.

Below: A double-page spread
from the Northern Telecom
brochure, designed by Peter
Crowther for The Team. The
images were created using
Swivel 3D, MacroMind 3D and
Photoshop software.
Courtesy: Peter Crowther.

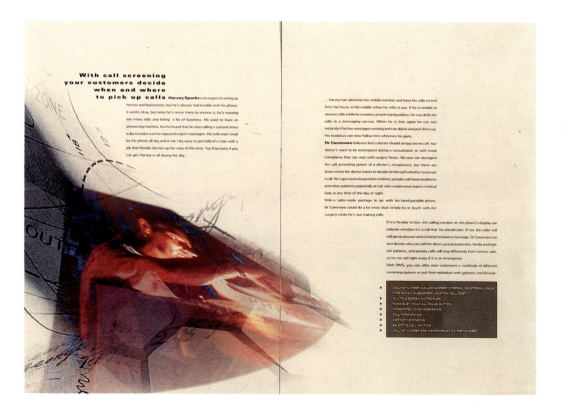

When Zanders Feinpapiere AG commissioned London-based design group 8vo to design their 1992 calendar, 8vo based their theme for the calendar around the measurement of time and the human understanding of timescales. The title is 'Time Machine Future', making reference also to Zanders new PM 3 advanced paper-making machine.

The whole calendar was designed on the Macintosh, using mainly FreeHand software and the original images combine art directed photography with pictures from image banks like the Science Photo Library.
Courtesy: 8vo, London.

Top: Metallic paper page, with machine image solarized on the Paintbox, lifting to reveal October.

Bottom: August lifting to reveal September.
Courtesy: 8vo, London.

items. Projects that might have once taken days are now produced in hours, which means increased capacity for the studio, greater profitability, and above all, a stimulating environment for designers.

A typical interface provided to the computer-aided designer allows for the interactive input of artwork, perhaps in the form of freehand sketches, together with a wide range of drawing aids for creating circles, ellipses, lines, rectangles, flexible curves, texture patterns, and drop shadows. These can be manipulated with different line thicknesses, colour, transparency, and multi-layering. Add to these features the ability to import images from other packages, artwork from scanners and colour copiers, and text in hundreds of typefaces, and one quickly appreciates the potential of these systems in the hands of a skilled designer.

Perhaps one of the major benefits of any computer-aided design system is the flexibility it offers designers. For nothing is ever really final – there is always time to try out another colour combination, a different format or font, introduce another image, or even leave items out until the very last moment, and then introduce them just before printing. Gone are the days when real paint, permanent ink or dry-mount letters froze an idea and restricted further experimentation simply because of

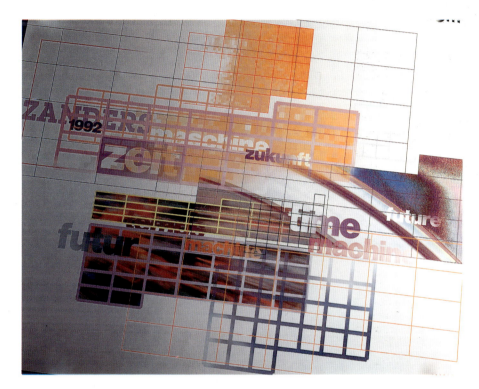

To create the cover, 8vo scanned an A4 laser print of the Macintosh visual into the Paintbox and used it as a template on which they reassembled elements from the calendar pages. The text and grids were typeset conventionally and scanned into the Paintbox.
Courtesy: 8vo, London.

November features a humming bird and the Z° particle which were combined on the paintbox. A metallic bronze and special pink were used in printing.
Courtesy: 8vo, London.

The Queen's 40th Anniversary 24p value stamp and first day cover were created by Why Not Associates. The type was created in FreeHand and the Paintbox used to combine the type and images.
Courtesy: By Permission of Royal Mail.

the time involved. The computer's virtual world of colour, shape, and space removes such pressures from the designer, who can investigate the relative merits of myriad possible solutions.

CASE STUDY: THE COMPUTER IN A GRAPHIC DESIGN STUDIO

The historic village of Theale, Berkshire, does not seem an obvious location for the headquarters of a computer-based design company. However, today's computer and communication technology releases many companies from the geographical constraints that hindered previous generations; which is why Spark Sales Promotion Ltd is able to offer a national design service, and still enjoy the benefits of an idyllic country setting.

Mike Vince, the Creative Director, has been with the company since its founding in 1991, and was instrumental in selecting the hardware and software that complements traditional design techniques. The hardware used by the company is Apple Macintosh, with a variety of software packages that include Aldus FreeHand and PageMaker, Adobe Photoshop, and Letraset's ColorStudio.

The company offers a wide range of professional design services for the printing of brochures, posters,

Puma UK commissioned Paterson Jones to design a brochure for their Young Puma sportswear collection. The page layouts were put together on an Apple Macintosh, using Aldus FreeHand. While the colour schemes were being finalized, outline designs of the garments were input and juxtaposed to contrast different colour combinations. Within a very short period of time of receiving the season's colour schemes, colour codes were assigned to the computer files which were then given to the printer to prepare the final colour separations for printing.
Courtesy: Paterson Jones Ltd.

This illustration was part of a large sales campaign for Richards. The original photograph was scanned, at a resolution of 300 dpi, into Letraset's ColorStudio. It was then posterized into two values before being stretched using Aldus PageMaker. Then, 10-inch by 8-inch negatives were produced from the disk files which were then used for silk-screen printing. *Courtesy: Richards and Spark Sales Promotion Ltd.*

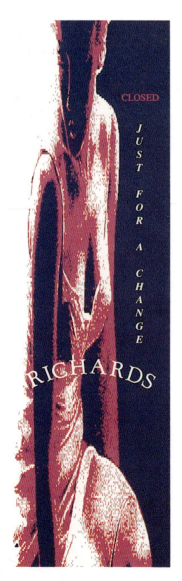

coupons, packaging, point of display, exhibitions, pamphlets and large corporate prospectuses. Although the computer plays an important role in the creative design process, Mike insists that it is only used when it offers creative and cost-effective reasons for its use.

One of the obvious advantages of using computers for graphic design is the flexibility it gives a designer for evaluating different typefaces in a project. No longer is it necessary to prepare original artwork to discover the impact a particular font has upon the visual message behind an image. The virtual nature of digital type means that a proposed design can be viewed on screen with different typefaces from a choice of several hundred.

The scanner is a valuable piece of hardware for the input of logos and other artwork that eventually become composited with computer-generated elements. However, although the small low-resolution systems play an important role, they cannot compete with the high-resolution systems that are still needed to capture photo-realistic images. Fortunately, it is relatively easy to hire scanning and imagesetting services from a bureau.

All of Spark's customers receive their first visuals in the form of a thermal print, which provides them with an accurate guide to the design in terms of

colour, resolution, size and visual accuracy. Final
artwork is either delivered in the form of a computer
disk from which colour separations are made, or in
the form of 10-inch by 8-inch negatives.

   Many projects are designed completely with the
Apple Macintosh computers, but this only happens
when there is an obvious design solution from
beginning to end. Mike Vince is adamant about the
role of the computer in his studios:

> 'It offers amazing solutions to some problems,
> but one must learn when and when not to use
> them. One could never abandon photographs,
> sketches, drawings, negatives and well-
> established printing processes. The computer is
> just another tool, albeit very powerful, and its
> ability to integrate input, design and output
> processes must never be underestimated.'

Digital computer technology has enabled companies
like Spark to quickly establish a reputation for
providing a low-cost design service with a rapid
response time, where design quality is never
compromised. For although today's hardware and
software can appear superficially seductive, Mike
Vince's advice to any designer working with
computers, is to always remain a designer.

3

50

G I R

B
VI S
A

Y

'He who first shortened the labour of copyists by device of Movable Types
was disbanding hired armies and cashiering most Kings and Senates, and
creating a whole democratic world: he had invented
the art of printing.'

THOMAS CARLYLE

3 Type & Print

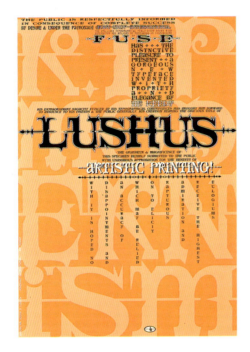

'LushUS' typeface and poster designed by Jeffrey Keedy, commissioned by FontShop International GmbH, for *Fuse* (Issue 4, 'Exuberance'). The typeface, in PostScript type 1 format, was designed using Fontographer and the poster was created in FreeHand and output straight to film. *Courtesy: Phil Baines.*

Left: A detail from a section divider from *Next Directory No. 7*, designed by Why Not Associates using FreeHand on a Macintosh. *Courtesy: Why Not Associates* for Next Directory No. 7.

EARLY BEGINNINGS

For almost two thousand years we have been searching for a technology to communicate the written and printed word, and the computer is only another solution to this process. However, computers have not been the only key to the latest technological revolution: lasers have provided an incredible tool for capturing print on paper, bromide and film. Together, computers and lasers have transformed the world of type and print, and together they have been responsible for the highest quality images ever produced by machines.

The letterforms in use today have been passed down from one civilization to another over hundreds, if not thousands, of years. Shapes have been corrupted, modified, misinterpreted, hybridized, distorted, and elaborated to a point where there are now thousands of ways of writing the letter 'A'. Even contemporary typeface designers have no difficulty in creating new shapes. Typefaces, like any other image, are subject to the whim of fashion; what was acceptable yesterday can appear outmoded today. Different typefaces are required for many applications. It is not just the world of books and newspapers that requires type styles – specialist fonts are required for posters, logos, signs, road markings, menus, invitations, poems, and car names.

Signs of Type

Emigre Graphics Type Catalog

A typeface is not incidental. Each generation of designers demands a choice of styles to complement the messages they wish to communicate. A typeface, with its personal characteristics, influences the reader's interpretation of the message. There are books and newspapers that unwittingly broadcast a message of 'don't read me – there isn't time', whereas others entice readers into their pages. This seduction is a skilled process and is central to the typographer's craft. Its success is a combination of expert knowledge of kerning, point size, letter, word and line spacing, x-height, and indents and margins, that collectively determine the mood or atmosphere of a page of text. Good typography enables the printed word to transmit its message to the reader without hindering the reading process; it must never come between the eye and the message. If the typography is seen, it has failed in its task.

There are times, however, when a graphic designer employs type as a graphic element, and deliberately invites the reader's eye to explore their image to discover hidden patterns and shapes. These are real sensitivities, and the world of type and print has just cause to react to any technology that ignores the accumulated knowledge of centuries, but in spite of some early misdemeanours, the computer is more than making up for the innocent abuse of the typographer's domain. Computer and laser technology now competently handle every serif, each consistent letter stroke, subtle kerning, and the integration of text with graphics. These achievements have only become possible through several simultaneous developments. Computer processors are now reasonably cheap; high-resolution bitmapped displays are commonplace; and lasers have been harnessed to play their fine coherent light beams over paper, bromide and film.

The reason for the computer's success in the

world of type and print is that many features of Gutenberg's press have been replaced by software and digital hardware. The character dies have been replaced by numerically digitized shapes. The matrix has been replaced by computer memory which holds the codes representing the text. The lead has been substituted by digital signals and finely balanced laser optics, and operations such as hyphenation, centering, justification, kerning and line spacing are all tasks now undertaken by software. However, where metal type changes the design of the font according to size, in computers the same cut of font is used for every size.

But the computerization process has not stopped here: there are features for headlines, rotating letters, spelling checkers, indexes, tables, graphics, page numbering, headers and footers, widows and orphans; the list is endless. Such flexibility, though, has its own dangers, especially in the hands of naïve users operating a desktop publishing system for the first time. With so many menus to choose from and so many parameters to modify, the flexibility can overwhelm the inexperienced operator who is tempted to use them all at once or ignore them. But before examining the world of desktop publishing, perhaps the virtual world of computer type and print should be reviewed.

Above and left: Examples from
The Emigré Catalog.
Used in *Emigré* magazine,
which was founded in 1985 by
Rudy VanderLans, the
typefaces are designed by
Zuzana Licko on a Macintosh
using Fontographer.
Courtesy: Emigré.

The top diagram shows how
three points – A, B and C –
are used to form a Bézier
curve. Points A and B define
the start and end positions
for the curve whilst the point C
influences the intermediate
shape of the curve. In the lower
diagram, the control point C
has been moved and the
change it has caused in the
curve's form is clearly visible.

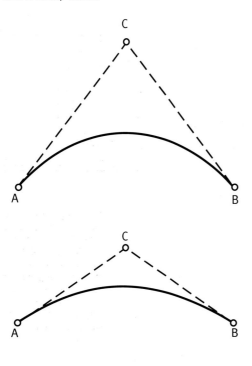

VIRTUAL TYPE

Two basic methods are used to represent the shape of a character: the first employs a bitmapped representation, where a rectangular grid is used to locate the bits forming the interior of the letter; and the second method uses an outline shape constructed from curve segments. Bitmapped fonts are only intended for dot matrix printers, laser printers and bitmapped screens, where their size remains fixed. However, the resolution of the outline technique is variable, as it depends upon how the laser-driven output device is set.

Although it is easy to visualize the individual dots that make up any bitmapped image, an outline format requires a little explanation. The digitizing process reduces a contour to a sequence of points that would be connected together by straight lines if plotted. This does not seem like a useful method for representing the outline of a letter, especially if it had delicate curves and fine serifs, but there is a similar technique that uses these points to develop smooth curves between them – these are called Bézier curves, after their inventor.

Pierre Bézier worked for Renault and developed a CAD system for designing smooth car panels by only specifying the position of a few 3D points, from which a computer program derived all other points on the surface. The technique has a 2D equivalent whereby a smooth curve can be derived from three or four guide points. Without introducing any mathematical support for this technique, it is possible to see, by referring to the illustration on the left, how a smooth curve can be drawn between points A and B using an intermediate point C.

It is possible to write a computer program which arranges that the point C acts like a magnet by attracting the curve towards it. The curve will only touch C if it is placed somewhere on a straight line joining A and B, otherwise it only acts as a controlling point – in fact it is often called a control vertex. If the point C is moved to another position the curve will form another path which enables an infinite number of curves to be created simply by changing its position.

By joining a number of these Bézier curves together, an outline of a letter can be created with only a few dozen coordinates, but the important point to remember is that these numbers encode one continuous curve which can be fine-tuned by adjusting the control vertices.

Outline fonts can be downloaded to a laser printer so that the software in the host computer only needs to supply the font name, its size, the requested letter and its position on the paper. Meanwhile, the bitmapped descriptions are used to display the shapes on the display screen.

For an outline form, a Raster Image Processor (RIP), which is a general-purpose computer processor, converts the shape into a collection of horizontal or vertical strips, whose thickness is determined by the selected laser resolution. The page is then created by building up the image from rasters that collectively create the individual letterforms.

Even small laser printers may require a few Mbytes of memory to hold these fonts, and to save

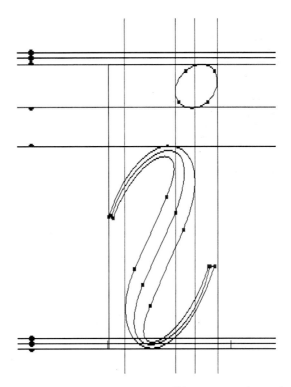

This computer printout shows the Bézier curves used to define the outline of a letter 'i' in Italian Book italic. The horizontal and vertical lines are the hinting links which guarantee that the letterform is mapped correctly to the output device's pixels.
Courtesy: The Electronic Font Foundry Ltd.

56 time in the rasterization process, inactive time is used to convert frequently used font outlines into their raster format ready for the printer's next user. It would be difficult to store hundreds of typefaces in their raster form as this would consume vast amounts of memory, which is why special formats like PostScript and TrueType (see below) are used. However, in saving memory, the Raster Image Processor must spend time in converting outline shapes into high-resolution rasters.

A LANGUAGE FOR THE PAGE

One of the major benefits introduced by digital printing is the seamless blending of type with graphics. This requires a list of commands describing exactly how the composition is prepared, which is written in a Page Description Language (PDL) such as PostScript (developed by Adobe Systems Inc) or TrueType (developed jointly by Microsoft and Apple). A PDL accepts the specification of bitmapped and outline fonts; how characters are selected, sized, rotated and positioned; and how various patterns are created and composited with the text.

Scangraphic Visutek Limited have over 2,500 typefaces available for their imagesetters and have designed their own PDL to express the apparently

infinite number of ways in which text can be integrated with graphics. Their Scantext system enables a user to interactively develop the layout of a page which is seen and manipulated on a high-resolution screen. When completed, the system automatically develops a PDL script which, via the RIP, drives a high-resolution imagesetter. This machine houses the ubiquitous laser which, with the aid of a rotating glass prism 'sprays' its fine beam accurately over the bromide or film surface in a raster format. As these lasers cannot be switched on and off in thousandths of seconds, a crystal used for deflecting the laser is electrically modulated by the digital signals and diverts the beam from its normal path. It is this digital modulation that develops the accurate character outlines and fine halftone graphics. The laser's beam is incredibly fine (0.008 millimetres in diameter) and requires defocusing to develop the raster stripes that form the individual elements. But it is this fineness that permits resolutions in excess of 3,000 dpi to be achieved with great accuracy and consistency.

DIGITIZING TYPEFACES

A figure between 15 and 20 thousand is often quoted to describe the different fonts in existence. The definition of exactly what constitutes a font is slightly confused as some people classify an italic typeface as a separate font from its normal form, whereas others only classify the family style as the font. Nevertheless, there are still thousands of typefaces which often have individual interpretations by different type foundries.

Translating these letter shapes into a digital format is no easy task, as original typeface designs are held in various forms. These might be in the form of source drawings supplied to the typefounder, who

Janson

Janson

Many typefaces are named after their designers, and although Anton Janson worked in a type foundry in Leipzig, the original Janson matrices were cut by Nicholas Kis in the late 17th century. Monotype's Janson™ typeface is based upon the original matrices and preserves many of the original design characteristics.
Courtesy: The Monotype Corporation plc.

may have only used them as a guide, and virtually rendered the original designs worthless. Another source is from original metal type specimens and early film masters. These, too, have their problems as characters are often missing and sometimes flawed by shortcuts taken in their design. For example, many italic styles were produced by electronically sloping an upright typeface, which although was fast and automatic, introduced anomalies that are unacceptable today.

So faced with all of these problems, most typeface suppliers have been engaged upon an extensive programme of digitization. This basically involves a designer drawing on paper a complete set of characters to a height between 100 millimetres and 200 millimetres, which are then digitized by hand. The graphic design industry tends to use the Ikarus software package developed by URW in West Germany, which runs on a small graphics workstation.

Hand digitizing introduces its own level of errors, but these can be detected by the operator when the digitized shape is viewed upon a computer screen. Ikarus permits any point on the outline to be finely adjusted until the operator is satisfied that vertical and horizontal lines are true, curves and serifs are free from spurious wiggles, and stroke thickness is consistent. Ikarus can also be used to develop the kerning tables that control the space between a pair of letters such as 'We' and 'Yo'. Kerning is the name given to the creation of the optimum space between different pairs of letters, and is vital for the efficient interpretation of printed text. Today, there is no excuse for incorrect kerning – the typographer's expert knowledge can be captured in the form of tables which precisely specify the relationship between any pair of characters.

The digitization process can either represent a letter in the form of outline curves, which are very efficient in encoding this geometry, or in the form of bitmaps which construct each shape from a regular matrix of pixels. But no matter how they may be stored within the virtual world of the computer, what really matters is how the shapes eventually look on the printed page.

Although typefaces can be defined with mathematical precision, this in no way implies that vital characteristics are lost when a typeface is digitized. In fact, it is this precision that allows delicate nuances in curves to be captured. A good example is Monotype's Janson™ typeface (page 57) which dates back to 1690. The original Janson had a number of small irregularities which gave it a unique character and these have been incorporated into the latest digital version.

WHAT YOU SEE IS NOT WHAT YOU WANT (WYSINWYW)

One of the benefits of computer technology is the accuracy to which numbers can be stored; and as the outline of a letter employs x- and y-coordinates, they too can be stored to an accuracy measured in millionth's of inches or thousandth's of millimetres – an accuracy never before achieved. But no matter what the internal accuracy may be, unless the printing output device can resolve this fine level of detail, the extra accuracy is wasted. This leads to the situation where what you see is not what you want.

One device that is part of any computer system is the display screen which will probably have a resolution of 72 dpi. Obviously, this is incapable of resolving all of a typeface's fine detail. Indeed, internal bitmapped fonts are used to display text to maintain a high display speed, which means that what you see on the screen cannot be a perfect copy of what is printed if outline fonts are held in the laser printer. There are, however, software packages such as Adobe's Type Manager which enhances the quality of the screen typefaces by deriving the bitmaps from the rasterized outline fonts.

A popular acronym in desktop publishing is 'WYSIWYG' (pronounced Wis-i-Wig) which stands for 'What You See Is What You Get' and describes the graphical accuracy of information displayed upon the screen. Rather innocently it proclaims that 'what is seen on the screen is what is output'; this is not always strictly true, because the sampling natures of screens and laser printers are not equivalent. For high-resolution screens, however, it is a good approximation.

HINTING

Although the pixel nature of screens and laser printers provides a simple mechanism for displaying type and graphics, the sampling process does introduce unwanted aliasing artefacts in the form of jagged edges and irregular stroke thicknesses. However, these can be minimized by a process known as hinting. To understand the technique, consider the illustration on the right showing an outline font of a 12-point fullpoint greatly magnified. Here the outline description is positioned symmetrically over the pixel positions of the laser printer. But in the same illustration five other versions of the fullpoint are shown, where the outline is moved slightly. The general rule for making the pixel black is that if at least 50 per cent of a pixel is within the outline, then it becomes active.

Something as small as a fullpoint might not cause too much concern, but individual letters could become highly distorted, as illustrated on page 60 where six letter 'H's are displayed greatly magnified when unhinted. Therefore, to prevent characters from being distorted, extra information is required within the font descriptions to guide the computer making the final mapping to the laser's pixels. This information is in the form of guide-lines called 'links' or 'scaffold lines', which control the positioning of the outline shape upon the pixel surface.

The diagram at the bottom of page 60 illustrates

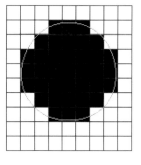

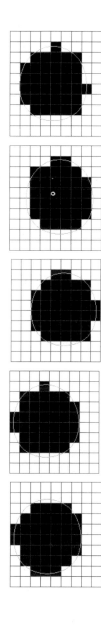

This illustration represents a 300 dpi bitmap of a 12pt fullpoint, greatly enlarged. The outline circle is the actual outline of the fullpoint, and when it is superimposed on the grid of pixels associated with the printed page, the only pixels filled are those that are at least 50% inside the outline. This fullpoint is correctly hinted, hence the symmetrical appearance. In this case, hinting guides the computer to slightly move the outline of the letterform so that it always appears at the optimum position on the grid of pixels and remains symmetrical.
Courtesy: The Electronic Font Foundry Ltd.

The series on the left shows what happens when a fullpoint is not hinted. The 50% sampling rule for activating pixels creates asymmetric shapes depending on the relative position of the outline.
Courtesy: The Electronic Font Foundry Ltd.

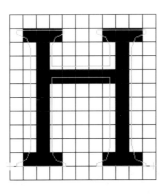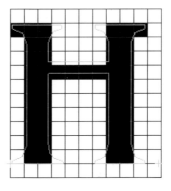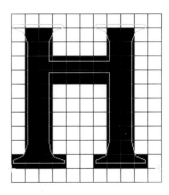

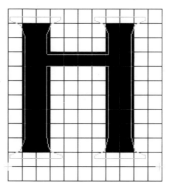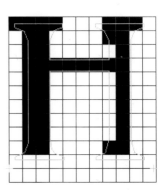

These six diagrams illustrate how a letter 'H' could appear if it was not hinted. By moving the outline very slightly over the grid of pixels, different pixels are activated.
Courtesy: The Electronic Font Foundry Ltd.

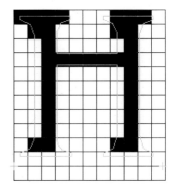

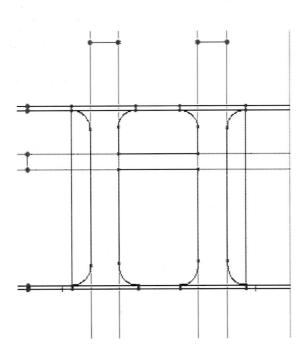

The hinting process employs connecting links (indicated by circular dots) to preserve the size of important features of the letter 'H'. The two uprights of the letter 'H' must always have the same thickness which is guaranteed by setting their links to the same width.
Courtesy: The Electronic Font Foundry Ltd.

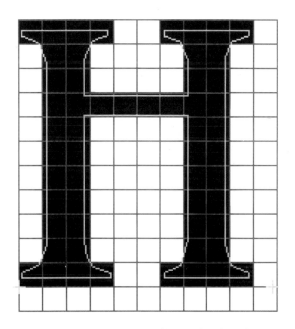

This greatly enlarged 90 dpi bitmap of a 12pt letter 'H' shows how hinting preserves the symmetry of the character, especially when dealing with fine serifs. Hinting is obviously vital when printing small type sizes at low output resolution. *Courtesy: The Electronic Font Foundry Ltd.*

the links needed to position the outline describing a letter 'H', and the diagram on the right of this page shows how hinting preserves the character symmetry.

VARIATIONS ON A THEME

So far the computer is simply providing another medium for handling letter shapes, and with the aid of laser printers produces high-quality output. But the computer's involvement does not stop here; once shapes are stored numerically they can be manipulated by a variety of mathematical and geometric processes. For example, having digitized and stored a typeface at 18 points (4.5 millimetres) it can be reduced in size by scaling its coordinates. This can adjust the typeface to any size within the range of the printing device. If we can scale down, then we can also scale up. However, the eye is not linear: optical relationships that hold for one scale do not necessarily hold for another. Translated into the world of type, this means that letter shapes and the surrounding white space that are acceptable as 12-point text are not acceptable when scaled to 36 points. In practical terms this means that different fonts are needed for text and headlines.

The need for two separate sizes is further compounded by the fact that small text fonts

Typography and Computer Graphics   0°

Typography and Computer Graphics   5°

Typography and Computer Graphics   10°

Typography and Computer Graphics   15°

Digital techniques make it possible to italicize text by the process of slanting, where the letterforms are allowed to lean away from the vertical by a small angle. Although this works for some fonts and small angles, the effect of slanting can make vertical strokes thinner and introduces unacceptable levels of distortion. In this example, the text is slanted in increasing angles of 5 degrees.
Courtesy: Scangraphic Visutek Ltd.

incorporate inktraps to assist the flow of ink during the final printing process. These would also be scaled up and introduce distortions into the headline text and therefore be unacceptable. A practical and professional solution to this problem is given by Scangraphic who provide two versions of each typeface: one for text which can be scaled up to 72 points – but the drawings are optimized for sizes up to 18 points (4.5 millimetres) – and the other for headlines which can be scaled to 380 millimetres.

Italics

In a computer scaling is nothing more than a multiplication operation, but another useful geometric operation is that of slanting to create italics. This process requires very simple mathematics to make a shape lean forwards or backwards, and is easily encapsulated within a program. Unfortunately, the further the shape leans over, the thinner the vertical strokes become. At small angles the thinning process is not so obvious, but for large ones the type can appear distorted. In spite of these drawbacks, this automatic process can be used to create the overall effect, and manually adjusted where unacceptable optical effects are introduced. Although slanting is available as an automatic process, for perfect results one must design a specific italic typeface.

Borders and shadows

Other typographic effects can be achieved automatically with software. And once these programs have been written, any typeface can be processed to create a wealth of new related fonts. For example, an original letter outline could be traced with lines of different thicknesses; the resulting shapes could even be made solid. Another effect is to trace a second line a fixed distance from the original, and perhaps incorporate a fill-in effect. The shape outline could be filled with various graphic embellishments or halftones, or even placed over some drop-shadow.

Interpolation

Interpolation is the process of deriving in-between (interpolated) shapes from two or more reference shapes. In typography, this means that given two different designs for a letter, software can create a family of related designs that trace the evolution of one shape into another. The process is easily understood by considering the action of a broad nib pen which can be used to create a range of writing styles depending upon the angle the nib makes to the line of writing. For example, if the pen's angle is 30 degrees, lines drawn along this angle are thin, while those drawn at 90 degrees to this direction are thick. This method of writing creates the familiar calligraphic italic style.

A similar effect can be created digitally by storing in a computer the strokes made by an imaginary pointed nib, where the writing angle has no effect. However, if the width of the nib is allowed to expand and contract horizontally during its journey along the calligraphic strokes, a solid letterform is created. This is called 'expansion', and the resulting ratio of thick to thin strokes is known as its 'contrast'.

When two original letterforms are stored in the Ikarus format it is possible to create new interpolated

Whenever a computer is used in design activities it frequently introduces new automatic processes that would have been impossible using traditional techniques. In these illustrations an original capital letter 'A' (top) from the bodytext font ITC Souvenir Bold has been automatically processed to create these embellished letterforms. They were created using batchfile processes available on the Scantext 2000 system.
Courtesy: Scangraphic Visutek Ltd.

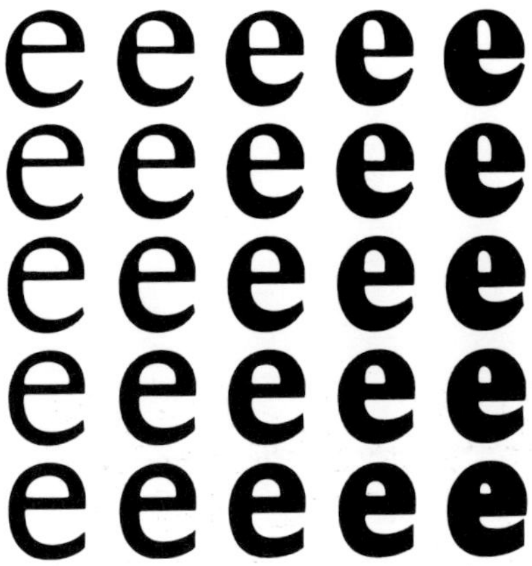

eeeee
eeeee
eeeee
eeeee
eeeee

The four corner letterforms
have been digitized and stored
in the Ikarus format. In the
horizontal direction the
interpolated in-between
letterforms show the effect of
different levels of expansion,
whilst in the vertical direction
the level of contrast is altered.
*Courtesy: Scangraphic Visutek
Ltd.*

letterforms showing different levels of expansion and contrast. For example, the illustration on the left shows 25 letters where only the four corner letters had to be digitized. And simply by interpolating the amount of expansion and contrast between these original shapes, a family of in-between shapes is created. It is only when one realizes that the same process can be applied to any letter of a typeface that one begins to appreciate the benefits of storing type digitally.

Special effects

If letters can be scaled, slanted and interpolated, then they can be subjected to any form of manipulation, given that a programmer can incorporate the equations within the software. This is more to satisfy the needs of a graphic designer than a typographer, who is traditionally constrained by the methods of printing type.

A graphic designer, on the other hand, may wish to explore the possibility of using text as a graphical element by relaxing the reader's eye from a horizontal scanning process and force it to explore other shapes and discover hidden visual messages. For example, text can be set upon an undulating base line, or it can be wrapped around a circle or even wound into a spiral. Achieving this effect manually could be impossible, as typefaces need to be distorted if the individual letters are not to touch one another; but with the correct software, subtle shaping can be applied very effectively.

Halftone

A standard laser printer with 300 dpi gives eight million pixels on an A4 sheet, and although this seems a large number, it is not sufficient to support fine halftone patterns. However, a high-quality laser recorder with a resolution exceeding 3,000 dpi can cover an A4 sheet with more than 800 million pixels, all of the same size. At this resolution, precise grey scales can be reproduced using halftones and incredibly fine text.

The halftones are created by selecting a suitable screen spacing, which may vary between 16 and 75 lines per inch (lpi), and placing a suitable size dot at each screen position. As the eye is efficient at detecting vertical and horizontal patterns, the screen is rotated by 45 degrees for monochrome images.

To reproduce a photograph using this process the original image is scanned in and sampled at this resolution; the tonal density of the sampled point determines the diameter of the dot placed on the halftone screen. As the dot diameter is ultimately responsible for the density of the output image, the computer can be used to manipulate the image in some way. Consider the case of scanning in a black-and-white photograph and storing the samples to 256 digital grey levels. A dramatic change to the output tonal range could be created by processing the image such that density levels between 0 and 100 are represented by one large dot; density levels between 101 and 200 have a medium size dot and the remaining levels have no dot at all. The picture has been reduced to three intensities: black, an intermediate grey, and white.

The variable size dots in this magnified portion of a halftone screen create the changes in tone, and for monochrome printing the entire grid is rotated through 45° to minimize the detection of vertical and horizontal banding.

When images are stored digitally a variety of image processing filters can be applied to them: in these examples, the original image (top) is unsharpened, while the one below has been enhanced by increasing its sharpness. *Courtesy: Scangraphic Visutek Ltd.*

Although this illustrates the process, one can also imagine how software can allow the designer to alter the dynamic range of an image by preserving the number of densities but altering their distribution. This is a powerful form of image processing and takes photography away from baths of developers and fixing agents into the computer's virtual darkroom where the only equipment is software.

Another useful feature is image sharpening. This involves the computer in investigating neighbouring pairs of pixels, and where a certain contrast ratio is detected it is increased by making one pixel darker and the other lighter. The process effectively enhances the highlights and shadows and aids the eye in identifying more detail.

Integrating graphics and type

Representing graphics as digital halftones and typefaces as Bézier outlines provides a perfect mechanism for integrating both elements within the computer. The user simply scans in the artwork at a suitable resolution and interactively composes tints, images and type upon a high-resolution screen. Text can be made opaque or transparent, or even reversed out to appear white on black. It can be made visible through parts of an image and composed in an infinite number of ways. Eventually, the user's final

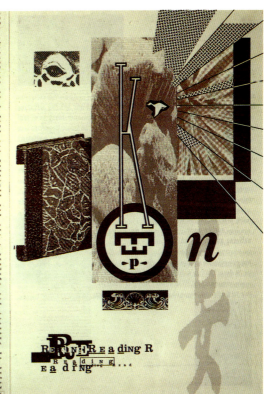

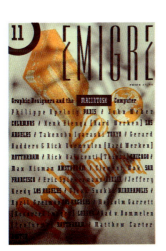

This page and page 68: *Emigré* magazine, founded in 1985 by Rudy VanderLans, is an exercise in experimental graphic design. The California-based magazine is designed using Macintosh software and employs a two-colour printing technique to achieve its unique style. The typefaces are designed by Zuzana Licko, using Fontographer.

Emigré uses software packages Ready, Set, Go!, FullPaint, MacVision and Fontographer. Publisher Rudy VanderLans discovered that programs such as Ready, Set, Go! would overlap type in a way that conventional typesetting could not; hence *Emigré's* dense layering trademark. *Courtesy: Emigré.*

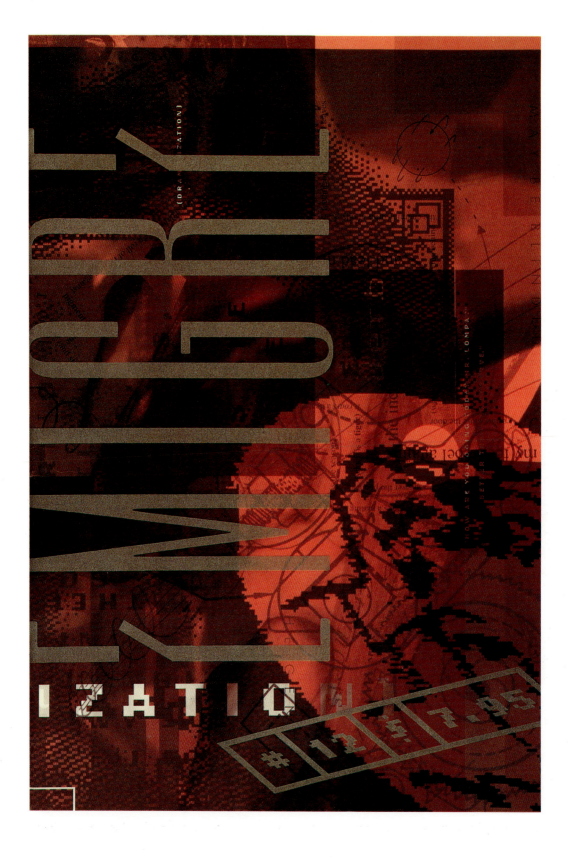

description is directed to the RIP which converts the overlays into a continuous halftone image.

Halftone colour

Any colour image can be scanned into a computer system and stored in an RGB or CMY digital format. During the scanning process the colour balance can be modified; perhaps the blue component is to be attenuated or the red component enhanced. Even the distribution of primary colour graduations can be altered to modify the colour contrast. However, once the image is in this format it can be manipulated using standard electronic painting techniques.

The image can be merged with type, graphical elements and other images, and when a final output is required it is processed to extract the cyan, magenta, yellow and black components, which are output as halftone colour separations on the laser imagesetter. The halftone colour separations are created such that they do not overlap one another, but are rotated through subtle angles to minimize the creation of moiré fringes (see Glossary). The beauty of this technique is that it is accurate, and capable of extremely high-quality printed pictures.

DESKTOP PUBLISHING

Desktop Publishing (DTP) systems did not suddenly break upon the computer scene; in fact, they have been evolving towards their current format for a quarter of a century. The original editing programs used by the first programmers provided primitive facilities for creating and correcting scripts of text. These evolved into simple word-processing programs which introduced the ideas of underlining, centering, justification, and pagination. In recent years, with the advent of dot-matrix and laser printers, word-processors reached a level of sophistication that met the requirements of the modern secretary.

Meanwhile, certain software houses identified the publishing market as future users of low-cost computer-based printing. Computers were becoming very fast, cheap enough to be purchased by the general public, and small enough to fit on a desk. Today, desktop publishing is transforming the way authors prepare manuscripts, architects submit tenders, managers prepare reports and corporate bodies communicate with their shareholders. Work that used to go to the local typesetter or printer is now undertaken in-house.

The Apple Macintosh computer and software products like QuarkXpress have virtually placed on a desk, Gutenberg's press together with access to a high level of typographical knowledge accumulated through the centuries – although some typographers may still view DTP systems with some suspicion. Such desktop publishing systems are extremely sophisticated: they incorporate in one environment the ability to design fonts, capture or import source text, integrate graphics with text and finally create high-quality printed documents.

DTP systems include parameters for selecting fonts, font size and style, kerning tables, leading values, x-heights, letter spacing, column widths and many more. All of these parameters have a profound

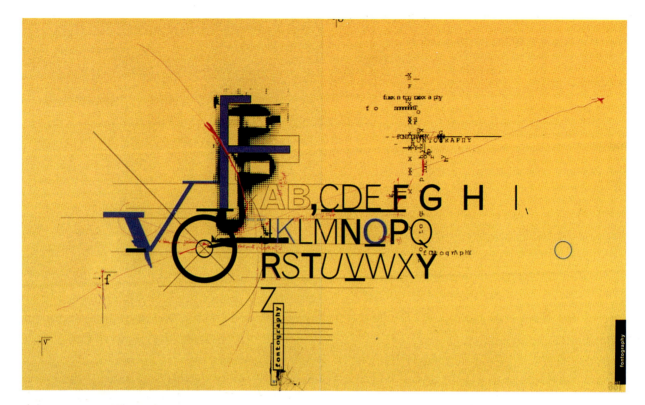

Photoshop, FreeHand and Applescan were employed by Why Not Associates to assemble this double-page spread for *Typography Now. See Bibliography for credits.*

Peter Crowther designed this NDL brochure cover on a Macintosh using Photoshop. Scanned images were montaged together in Photoshop adding depth and perspective. The typography was later applied in Photoshop.
Courtesy: Peter Crowther.

effect on the readability of the final text, its visual appearance and its success in allowing ideas and information to be transmitted to the reader. Casual users of DTP systems must be sensitive to the delicate relationships that exist between these parameters, otherwise they are ignoring all of the lessons that have been learnt over the centuries by typographers.

DATA STORAGE

One benefit of digital technology is the compactness with which information can be stored magnetically or optically. A single 3.5-inch computer disk easily holds 1Mb – which is equivalent to a small book – while a compact disk can store the equivalent of 250,000 A4 pages. Some national newspapers are already marketing compact disks which contain a full year's coverage of news items. Compact disks are also being used to distribute collections of their typefaces. A single CD can hold 1,000 fonts in Adobe's PostScript Type 1 format and provides a unique method of storing such valuable data.

APPLICATIONS

In a relatively short period of time we have witnessed the move from hot-metal typesetting to optical methods, and finally to digital typesetting. And although the importance of the RIP and the laser imagesetter must be recognized, the arrival of DTP systems is also highly significant.

Anyone who has access to a PC is able to undertake printing projects which only a few years ago required the involvement of a professional printer at an early stage. Nowadays, anything from a business card to a technical report can be designed in house before releasing a computer disk to a printer

'CanYou' typeface and poster by Phil Baines, commissioned by FontShop International GmbH, for *Fuse* (Issue 1 'Invention and Prophecy'). The typeface, in PostScript, was designed using FontStudio, converted to type 1 with Metamorphosis. Poster artwork was assembled conventionally using 300 lpi output from FontStudio as the pink background type, with high-resolution (purple) type set in PageMaker.
Courtesy: Phil Baines.

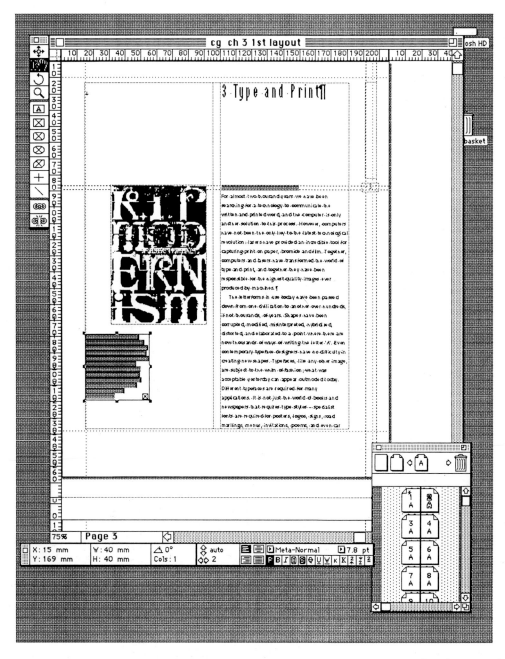

72

Page layouts – taken from this book – were created on QuarkXpress and the pictures were scanned in.

The flexibility offered by DTP systems means that changing page layouts and moving pictures is easy and because the type is linked and flows from page to page, editorial changes can be seen immediately in relation to the design.

who makes the final transfer to paper. The freedom and flexibility offered by DTP packages cannot be fully appreciated unless one has had the opportunity of discovering the ease with which different layouts can be tried; how typestyles can be visualized; and the effect that leading, column width, margins and justifications have upon the visual impact of a page. The computer enables all of these parameters to be explored within a DTP environment.

A graphic designer can, with the aid of a scanner, input logos, symbols and pictures and compose layouts incorporating text and graphics, which previously required scissors and glue. The computer's speed in responding to a designer's request means that the designer is able to pursue a design goal until it is achieved.

DTP is a massive market in virtually all walks of life. The high-street printing bureau equipped with a PC and DTP package, can offer a service to small businesses and the general public for all types of printed stationery. Publishers accept manuscripts from authors in electronic form, which can then be integrated with computer-generated artwork, and with the aid of a program application such as QuarkXpress, create the final negatives for the printing process. Local and national newspapers, and monthly magazines all benefit from DTP systems for the preparation of page layouts. And the ordinary business office which once employed antiquated typewriters to prepare long technical reports, manuals or documentation, now enjoy the new-found freedom of DTP systems.

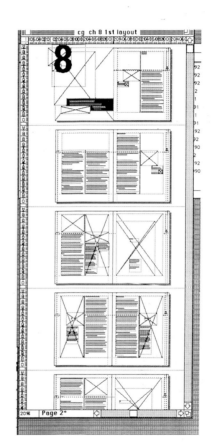

Another advantage of DTP systems is that pages can be viewed at different sizes; either greatly enlarged, or smaller so that several spreads can be seen at once.

CASE STUDY: DESIGNING 'ANTARA' – A DIGITAL TYPEFACE

This case study is based upon the final-year project submitted by Maria Quiroz for her Postgraduate

The labour of the writer
is the refreshment of the reader.
The one depletes the body, the other
advances the mind. Whoever you are,
therefore, do not scorn but rather be
mindful of the work of the one labouring
to bring you profit...If you do not
know how to write you will consider it no
hardship, but if you want a detailed account of
it let me tell you that the work is heavy:
it makes the eyes misty, bows
the back, crushes the ribs and belly, brings
pain to the kidneys, and makes
the body ache all over.
Therefore, O reader, turn the leaves gently
and keep your fingers away from the
letters, for as the hailstorm ruins the
harvest of the land so does
the unserviceable reader destroy
the book and the writing.
As the sailor finds welcome the final
harbour, so does the scribe
the final line

Dea gratias semper.

Postgraduate student Maria
Quiroz used Fontastic to
design the 'Antara' typeface
which was based upon her
own handwriting. It was
designed specifically for the 72
dpi resolution of the Macintosh
screen and the ImageWriter,
and conveys a convincing
sense of spontaneity.
Courtesy: Maria Quiroz.

Diploma in Graphic Design and Computers at Central St Martin's College of Art and Design (London). The aim of the project was to produce a cursive typeface based upon her own handwriting, to contrast with the more formal typefaces generally found in computer-based systems. Typefaces available for low-resolution output are often simply bitmap imitations of high-resolution designs, which introduces a significant compromise. Maria was dissatisfied with the polarization of the 'old traditions' and new technology, and was keen to discover ways of bringing them into closer contact. The equipment for her project consisted of an Apple Macintosh computer, an ImageWriter II and the Fontastic Plus software package.

Designing to a motif 'hamburgerfonstiv' the initial designs for the letters were prepared and digitized. However, these were 'stiff' and lacked the spontaneity that one normally associates with handwriting. It was only when Maria referred to text she had written in a free and unconscious way, that she discovered the level of detail and random features she wanted to incorporate into her design. Slowly but surely, she began to identify the features that would become a typeface called 'Antara'.

Designing to an 18-point height, each letter's bitmap was created on the screen. This was a slow process, as ways had to be discovered to introduce cursive detail that had to be defined as stroke widths on one bit. The maximum stroke width never exceeded two bits and holes were deliberately introduced to simulate the random breaks typical of handwriting.

After designing the lowercase letters Maria began work on kerning and character fit. Then the uppercase letters were designed and finally the complete alphabet was evaluated using sample text. Both English and Spanish text was used in this process, as

14

These two screen dumps show the individual bitmaps used to form the upper- and lower-case letterforms 'K' and 'k'. Note the design problems of creating fine calligraphic strokes from single pixels. A scaled version of the bitmap is displayed in the top left-hand corner of the screen's menu. *Courtesy: Maria Quiroz.*

Maria was interested to discover whether her own Peruvian origins would reveal whether her typeface was suited to the Spanish language rather than the English language.

Normally, most bitmapped type requires a bitmap for each point size, but 'Antara' was successful in a different range of sizes from 10 point to 18 point. However, the largest size does allow the cursive quality of the typeface to emerge.

Maria does not consider 'Antara' a script typeface; she simply wanted to retain the idiosyncracies of personal handwriting in a digital typeface and contribute to the 'vernacular' of typeface design.

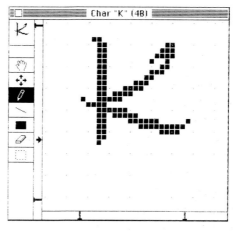

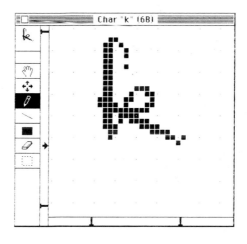

4

'Fashion, the arbiter, and rule of right.'

SIR RICHARD STEELE

4 Fashion & Textiles

Above: A selection of character prints, including Dennis the Menace and Popeye, by Courtaulds Fabric Prints. The ideas were developed using Computer Design Silicon Graphics Incorporated 2D software on Iris 3130 hardware.
Courtesy: Courtaulds Fabric Prints.

Left: A detail of work carried out by Sonia Jane Lester, a 1st-year HND Fashion Design Technology student at Cheltenham and Gloucester College of Higher Education.
Courtesy: Alan Villaweaver, Senior Lecturer and Faculty IT Coordinator.

THE FASHION WORLD

The fashion industry is a large and complex one and is in a continuous state of flux. Success is often measured in terms of whether any stock remains in the warehouse at the end of a season. Therefore, predicting those styles that will sell in large quantities is central to maximizing the turnover and profits of a fashion company.

The slightest disturbance to the fashion scene can trigger a wave of buying that no amount of planning can anticipate. A new film for the teenage community can overnight increase the sales of suitably decorated socks by millions of pairs. A celebrity photographed wearing a certain tee-shirt, pair of shorts or swimming costume can empty the shelves of that product in a matter of days, leaving frustrated customers, and clothing manufacturers regretting a missed opportunity.

Any manufacturing process which supports such a dynamic market must be highly flexible in its ability to respond to sudden changes, which is why computers play such an important role in this industry. Computer-based technology is available for every stage from original design, through manufacturing to retail, and it is the creative potential of computer graphics that is preparing the fashion industry for the twenty-first century.

These two images show how CAMEO Professional's fabric draping technique is used to overlay a new fabric. Note how the seam of the sleeve has been used to divide two pieces of the fabric, and how the original shadows have been preserved. The final image was output on a Canon Colour Laser Copier.
Courtesy: Winifred Aldrich, CAD Designer Services.

DESIGN CONCEPTS

A traditional low-tech method for representing new designs for any product is for the designer to draw on paper in either one or a combination of several media. An alternative approach is to use a high-tech method such as an electronic paint system on a computer. Using a computer can have many advantages. For example, an electronic image of a model dressed in a fashionable two-piece suit can be quickly prepared, and by manipulating the colour palette of the paint program, an extensive range of alternative colour combinations for the garment can be explored in seconds. A traditional drawing method cannot match the speed with which these extra visualizations can be produced on a computer.

Another computerized visualization technique allows new textile designs to be superimposed on photographs of existing garments. A photograph of a model wearing a garment is scanned into a paint system and displayed on the screen. The designer, with the aid of an interactive pen, traces around the border of the item of clothing which can then be filled with a substitute textile design. Although this mapping does not take into account the wrapping of the pattern about the body's shape, it does provide a useful first-level visualization. A further level of realism can be achieved by drawing onto the image extra lines which highlight the 3D form of the mannequin. When the fabric is then mapped onto the image, it is slightly distorted to simulate the effect of wrapping around the body. Even this is not completely accurate, but the discrepancies are so minor that the final visuals provide a very useful design tool.

Paint systems provide the designer with certain standard facilities such as the possibility of retouching the image to remove unwanted elements, or introducing features like shadows. Extra images can be composited with the original and the ensemble integrated with different backgrounds. The digital nature of the image enables hard copies to be quickly and cheaply output to ink-jet printers and colour laser copiers.

WOVEN FABRICS

Visualizing a woven fabric is a difficult process and requires considerable experience in order to predict the texture, colour and feel of the material. This is partly due to the variety of yarn types and weaving constructions that exist. There are single yarns consisting of a single thread, folded yarns where two or more threads are twisted together, and cabled yarns where two or more twisted yarns are further twisted together. There are also combination yarns, flat yarns, spun yarns, and straw yarns. When these form the warp and weft threads in a weaving process they produce fabrics including plain, whipcord, wincey, crêpe and cavalry twill. Add to this the fancy yarns such as spiral, gimp, loop, snarl, knot, stripe, eccentric and slub which give other textural effects, and the complexity of the subject becomes apparent.

Prior to the computer, the only way of discovering what these weaves would look like was to manufacture a piece of the material. Current software

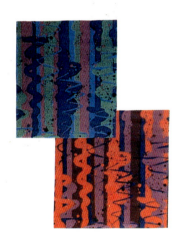

These print ideas for menswear and boyswear were developed using Computer Design Silicon Graphics Incorporated 2D software on Iris 3130 hardware. The colour variations were produced on the system and scanned onto garment shapes to give simulated garments in the print before the print was produced on the actual fabric. *Courtesy: Courtaulds Fabric Prints.*

tools enable the textile designer to simulate the construction of a woven fabric within a computer. The final visualizations are very effective and can be displayed as true-size images. The screen image cannot replace a textured piece of material, but it is very effective as a means of appraising potential new weaves. The design computer can also be directly connected to a computer-controlled loom in order to produce a woven sample.

Courtaulds Fabric Prints developed this pattern, using Computer Design Silicon Graphics Incorporated 2D software, to illustrate how the background of a fabric can change from white to black to create alternative colourways. *Courtesy: Courtaulds Fabric Prints.*

PRINTED TEXTILE DESIGN

Paint systems provide an excellent medium for developing new textile designs for print. The design of a repeated motif is straightforward: the designer selects a colour from the palette and begins colouring the screen's pixels. As with all painting programs, the operator can zoom in to any area of the design and make precise adjustments to any individual pixels.

An alternative to this approach is to scan in a coloured design and then work on it on the computer screen. This method usually requires the designer to reduce the number of colours scanned in to a manageable number (the scanning process generates many different shades and hues). Suitable software can select and alter specific colours and show the design in a reduced palette. If this colour combination is not satisfactory the designer can use the computer system to explore any other palette of colours. A very sophisticated level of flexibility is available from the appropriate software packages.

When the design is completed, a portion of the fabric can be displayed and various repeat layouts and offset arrangements can be explored. Simulated stitching and shadows can be introduced to add to the level of realism. Appropriate designs can then be printed out on paper, and it is at this stage that accurate colour control becomes important.

Colour control

Colours which can be stored inside a computer can be described as mixtures of red, green and blue (RGB), or cyan, magenta and yellow (CMY). When they are printed using a laser copier or colour printer, a translation occurs from a 'virtual' colour space to a 'physical' one. The physical colour space is determined by the printing mechanism and the inks or dyes used in the printing process. For example, it does not matter if a computer can store 16 million colours in its 'virtual' colour space; if the printer can only resolve 256 of them (the 'physical' colour space) the rest are lost. The computer industry does not, as yet, support a universal standard for the control of colour, so individual users must employ their own devices to handle their own special requirements.

In the case of a textile design, the designer may work with a colour palette chosen by the client, which may be a selection of Pantone colours or yarn samples. Ideally, the designer would like to work with these colours on the screen and print them out onto paper. In practice, however, the colours seen on a monitor depend on how the monitor's brightness, contrast and colour controls have been set, and other factors such as the ambient lighting levels of the room. The emphasis is placed, therefore, on getting them right at the printed output stage.

To achieve realistic colour prints a series of colour samples are first printed out in the form of a colour chart, together with the computer's RGB or CMY levels for each one. A yarn is then matched against these samples and the best match selected. The colour palette of the paint program is then formed from the RGB or CMY values of the chosen colours, and the designer can continue the painting process with the knowledge that when a hard copy is finally produced, the colours will be very similar to those of the original yarns. If the printer is changed for a different technology, a new range of colour samples must be produced.

Not all colours can be created by mixing levels of red, green and blue. Experiments have shown that some colours cannot be matched without subtracting a colour component. To overcome this the CIE Colour Space was developed in 1931 by the Commission Internationale de l'Eclairage. It was based upon the results of experiments in which a large number of people were studied to discover how they perceived and described colours. The CIE Colour Space employs three hypothetical primaries for red, green and blue which, when combined, produce the gamut of visible colours. If the CIE primaries are used as an internal model for representing colours then each output device, whether it be a monitor, laser printer or

SOLID

LIQUID

Sonia Jane Lester, a 1st-year HND Fashion Design Technology student at Cheltenham and Gloucester College of Higher Education, produced these images using Drawmouse software.
Courtesy: Alan Villaweaver, Senior Lecturer and Faculty IT Coordinator.

ink-jet plotter, can be assigned a suitable interface for standardizing colours. However, unless self-calibrating monitors are used, changing the monitor's controls will still alter what the designer sees on the screen and what is finally printed.

COLOUR PRINTING

Paint systems can be used to develop and visualize preliminary designs, from which the final one will be selected. The ability to explore different colour combinations provides valuable time-saving advantages over manual methods. By scanning in different samples of plain material the coloured image can be seen superimposed upon real textures. This is a simple mechanism for enhancing the realism of the synthetic image.

KNITTING

Current knitting machines have digital interfaces that allow them to be driven by small computers. Such computers permit a designer to create an original design on a screen which will then directly drive the knitting machine to produce the garment or fabric. This is a quick and effective method of developing knitting samples.

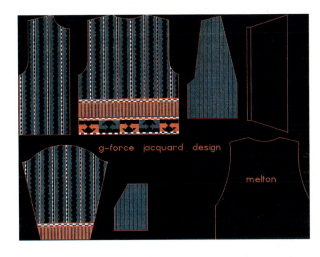

This jacquard design is part of a 3rd-year knitwear project by Gaynor Travena at Nottingham Polytechnic, in conjunction with G-Force of Nottingham and their knitwear design consultant, Gail Sallis. The students were required to use CAD/CAM not only to produce their finished products but also to generate their portfolio illustrations and specification sheets. The students used ORMUS Fashion System software.
Courtesy: Brenda Sparkes, Nottingham Polytechnic.

Top: The Fish Fairisle and Van Gogh CAD print socks were produced on a CDI, using PC-based software which has basic colour graphics, a Howtek Scanner and an A4 Canon Ink-jet Printer.
Courtesy: Courtaulds Socks.

Bottom: These floral-design knitted-socks are shown with their computer originated artwork. They were also produced using the system outlined above.
Courtesy: Manufactured by Courtaulds Socks exclusively for Marks & Spencer Ladies Hosiery Department.

Visuals play an important part in convincing the client of the effectiveness of a design. For example, if the client has given a brief for socks, they will want to see how different sock sizes look with the same decoration and how the product will look in its final packaging. This can be achieved quickly and effectively on a computer, and then printed out for the client to see.

3D MODELLING

Computers represent 3D objects as easily as 2D shapes. As the fashion industry gains more confidence with technology, it will use this technique more. The computer can show a 3D mannequin on which a garment can be superimposed. Texture mapping can be used to decorate the fabric. The texture map will be a real or synthetic material pattern which can be painted by the computer onto the garment.

Using a modern graphics workstation, the 3D model can be illuminated and rotated and thus seen from any direction. Looking towards the future, there is nothing to prevent the computer from creating real-time animations of a synthetic model dressed in next season's fashions walking on the screen. Their bodies would move realistically, their arms would swing and their clothes would move accordingly, and a simulated breeze could be used to add an extra level of realism. This might seem far-fetched, but it already exists in a non real-time mode, therefore it is only a question of the arrival of faster computers to make it all happen in real-time.

However, the above scenario could leave the fashion designer with an excellent visualization, but no means of transferring the concept into a practical example. In order to proceed to manufacture, patterns must be constructed.

PATTERN DESIGN SYSTEMS

Although it is easily demonstrated, it is not always appreciated that in general a 2D surface cannot be mapped onto a 3D free-form object without creasing or tearing. For example, a piece of wallpaper can be easily pasted over flat walls without splitting or creasing; even cylindrical objects such as pillars can be papered; but try any other type of surface and the paper will tear or crease. Garments are almost all cut from flat (2D) fabric and are formed by joining individual pieces together. Pattern cutters are used to transforming shapes from 2D to 3D and back again in their desire to achieve good fit.

Cutting the individual pattern pieces needed for any garment is a complex and skilled process. Ideally the pattern shapes should be derived from the person's body destined to wear the final garment, but in today's world of low-cost clothes and mass markets such processes are impossible, apart from at the level of haute couture. Standard sizes (eg womenswear size 10, 12, 14 and so on) are used to provide tables of body measurements for general use. Garments are usually designed for one of these standard sizes (eg 12) and the pattern pieces are then used as templates for creating the other sizes in the range. This process is known as 'grading'. Sample garments or 'toiles' are usually made before anything is put into mass production.

Once the pattern pieces have been created for the complete range of sizes the cloth has to be cut. The process of 'lay planning' is used to minimize the amount of material that will be wasted when the garments are cut out. The processes of grading and lay planning have been available on computer systems for some time.

Pattern cutting has also been computerized, although early systems did not appreciate the level of skill needed by the pattern cutter. This meant that the operator of the computer-based system had to be skilled in pattern cutting, and also had to understand a sophisticated menu-driven computer graphics system. Consequently they were not widely embraced by the industry. Nevertheless, they are, in the right hands, a powerful design tool, which, given the right user-friendly interface, will become a standard feature in the world of fashion.

One of the dangers of computerizing any process, be it clothes design or car design, is just to translate existing manual procedures into computer procedures. It is highly likely that existing methods for designing or manufacturing anything are dictated by the available machinery, tools and materials. Given a fresh start with different technology, new and innovative processes can be discovered which remove can be output and input to the remaining manufacturing process.

The digital nature of the data means that the computer can assist in other ways. For example, the computer can be programmed to supply the total area of the fabric needed for different garment sizes. It could also compute the length of stitching needed to fabricate the garment. It could even be used to output the vital alignment marks to ensure that patterns and material bias are respected during the final fabrication.

COMPUTERS EVERYWHERE

Computers are not only being used in the early stages of design and visualization, they are also used to control machinery in manufacture. In fact, in the clothing industry, their main use has been in manufacturing. Computer software can assist in lay planning, which determines how patterns can be organized to minimize wastage of material, and then computer-controlled water-jet cutters can use the optimized pattern layouts to cut the garment pieces. Computer techniques also assist in grading patterns to the range of commercial sizes.

Another area in which the computer can offer assistance is the cost control of garments, which is vital to the fashion industry. When any manufacturing process is computerized it implies that it can be accurately controlled. This means that when an integrated computer system is implemented, procedures and processes can be monitored which provide valuable data for evaluating the real cost for manufacturing garments.

It would be wrong to suggest that all of the above processes are widely employed throughout the fashion world, but the fashion industry certainly regards computer technology with a positive attitude.

the tedium and restrictions from traditional practices.

It could be that the knowledge we now have of 3D computer graphics systems can be transferred to the fashion industry and can provide pattern cutters with a truly interactive environment, where they can develop their patterns from a mannequin. Systems already exist where a 3D digitizer captures the surface topology of a model form and stores it within the computer as a collection of x-, y-, and z-coordinates. This model can then be displayed from any point of view upon the screen of a graphics workstation.

Like other computer-based modelling procedures, the operator interacts with the computer system by specifying the shape and line of different pieces of the garment's surface, and the system responds by developing a synthetic 'skin' for the model form. (It must be remembered, however, that garments are not actual 'skins', but hang from the body.) Seams are marked, together with pockets and the line of the garment. Then the system takes individual pattern pieces and attempts to flatten them, but as we know that this is impossible without tearing or creasing the surface, it attempts the transformation and highlights the areas of distortion using coloured zones. These are then used by the operator to relax the shape by opening up the darts and pleats. Finally, the patterns

Computers have a valuable contribution to make to the fashion industry, from the initial concept to the retail operation. And like so many disciplines that have benefited from computer technology, it would be unthinkable to consider the fashion industry without their involvement.

CASE STUDY: CAD IN A SMALL DESIGN STUDIO

Low-cost computer graphics systems based on PCs contribute to much of the success enjoyed by small design studios working in fashion, graphic design, typeface design, interior design and animation. One such company, owned by Winifred Aldrich, is CAD Designer Services based in the Nottingham Fashion Centre in the UK, who offer a range of services to textile and clothing manufacturers.

The two-person company owns four computer systems, but these do not dominate the workspace or dictate the working practices. Winifred Aldrich thinks that many companies installing computers do not always understand that the workbench space required for planning and presentation work should not change when computers are installed. It is totally counter-productive to relocate designers and computers in special rooms that are isolated from other daily design activities.

The four IBM-compatible computer systems are different in size and capability. However, it is the graphic cards in each which dictate the resolution and colour quality of much of the work that each can produce. Two systems work with super VGA cards at an 800 by 600 resolution, another has an 8-bit card with 1,024 by 768 resolution, and the latest addition has a 24-bit card with a 1,280 by 1,024 resolution. This full-colour system has made a dramatic difference to the quality and range of work that can be undertaken. Winifred finds it quite baffling to see companies using expensive systems to create simple colourways which could be as easily produced on simple, inexpensive PCs.

The customer is only marginally concerned with what is on the screen, it is the hard-copy output that is important. Most of the work is printed out on a Mitsubishi A3 thermal printer which combines quality with speed. At particularly busy times, as many as 70 prints have to be produced in a day, and those designs that have photographic or 'wash' effects are output to a Canon Colour Laser Copier using a local bureau service. An A0-sized pen plotter is used for the output of garment patterns and grades on card or paper; it is also used for some linear textile work.

A variety of software is used by the company and

These fine detailed images are examples of how computers can be used to handle the delicate qualities of lace. This early realization of designing lace shows how the original design is prepared using various motifs in the form of a line drawing (top), from which the computer is used to develop a visualization (bottom).
Courtesy: Winifred Aldrich/Guy Birkin, CAD Designer Services.

includes CAMEO Professional, Ormus Fashion, Ormus Hi-Res, CAMEO Paint, Coreldraw and Ventura.

When the company was formed in 1989, it expected to concentrate on garment design and pattern cutting, but in fact most of the work has been in textile design, or decorated garment design. Samples of a range of designs are shown in the illustrations for this chapter.

Some of the work, for example lace simulation, has been undertaken in response to client demand. This is always a gamble; the experiment may prove fruitless, but the challenge is tempting.

The studio's design work for large client companies has centred on marketing designs because the large fabric printers produce their own colour separations. Small clothing companies usually use one of the many small printers in the area. These companies will usually require both the artwork and the colour separations.

There has been an explosion of decorated leisure wear, but competition is fierce and the profit margins on short production runs are small, therefore the design work has to be fast and affordable. Winifred believes that the larger companies will use a small studio because its speed and personal service can reduce their response time.

She also holds the opinion that working for large

companies does include a hazzard. The better the work produced for this type of customer by the studio, the more likely it is that the studio will lose that customer, because they too see the benefits of the technology and may purchase a similar system.

There are, however, many large companies who do not wish to take on the responsibility of owning CAD equipment, or fear being left in a vulnerable position if trained staff subsequently leave. This has led to client designers coming to CAD Designer Services to hire time on the systems, only paying for technical support where required. Other designers come in and direct a design process but leave the technical work to the studio.

CAD Designer Services in Nottingham offer a range of services to textile and clothing manufacturers, including printing out designs for clients. Although this image of sweatshirts has a raster format, its high resolution enables line detail to be realized without unwanted aliasing.
Courtesy: Winifred Aldrich, CAD Designer Services.

'Television? The word is half Latin and half Greek.
No good can come of it.'
C. P. Scott

5

5 Television Graphics

CRYSTAL GAZING

It is almost certain that anyone who witnessed the first dim flickering images created by John Logie Baird in 1926 could not have seen the ramifications of his invention. How could any mind have extrapolated such a primitive technology into what we take for granted as television today? Who could have foreseen that one day the human race was to witness live pictures broadcast to the earth from the surface of the moon? And yet television has now become a vital and integral part of our lives.

Television has also become the major channel of communication for mass audiences. The average family returning home from school or work turns to the television as a means of relaxation or mental diversification, and a large percentage of the human race is prepared to sit motionless in front of a cathode ray tube and be seduced by soap operas, detective stories, comedy programmes, current-affairs programmes and news bulletins. Recent surveys have reported that some people can spend approximately 25 per cent of their waking lives staring passively at a television set.

Baird could not have seen the effects television would have upon human behaviour, nor could he have predicted the intersection between the technologies of television and computers. Computers were still passing through their mechanical phase when Baird was experimenting, and no inventor could have seen the evolutionary path that electronic technology was to take.

It was not until the 1970s that the cathode ray tube became an integral part of computer terminals. And it was towards the end of this decade that certain inventive minds married the processing power of the digital computer with video circuits. It was the tenacity of a few technologists that gave modern television its sophisticated image-processing facilities.

THE PIXEL IS BORN

With the benefit of hindsight, it is easy to see the natural marriage between computers and television; on the one hand there are images formed from discrete pixels (albeit very many) and on the other hand there is a computing environment whose digital nature makes the storage of millions of numbers an easy task. However, television has always been an analogue technology, as signals representing the luminance (brightness) and chrominance (colour) of a single raster are broadcast as a waveform rather than individual pixel attributes. Nevertheless, it is the discreteness of the displayed image that provides the common link between television and the computer.

Television technology exploits features of the human visual system to create animated coloured images; the persistence of the eye enables flicker-free animated images to be seen by displaying a number of discrete images every second. The NTSC (National Television Standards Committee) system employed in the USA uses 30Hz (cycles/second), while the PAL (Phase Alternate Line) system, used in the UK is 25Hz. This image refreshing mechanism is also employed in computer graphics systems. It is interesting to note that both of these refresh frequencies are based upon the frequency of the alternating electrical current in the different countries. If the electrical mains frequency was 50Hz and the television refresh rate 45Hz, the two frequencies would beat together and cause a 5Hz modulation of the picture; for this reason, the two frequencies are kept equal.

A sensation of colour is experienced when different combinations of red, green and blue light are seen. This phenomenon is exploited in the manufacture of television cathode ray tubes which use a regular matrix of red, green and blue phosphor dots which are individually excited by three separate electron beams. The phosphor also possesses a degree of persistence to help prevent the images on the screen from flickering.

Because of the discrete nature of television pictures, any image can be stored digitally by holding the colour primaries of each pixel in a block of computer memory or upon magnetic or optical disk. However, this is not the way a picture is encoded for broadcasting. When colour television was introduced, it had to be compatible with the existing monochrome service. Furthermore, special encoding methods had to be used to prevent colour transmissions from using a wide frequency bandwidth, otherwise one colour broadcast station would have been equivalent to three monochrome broadcast stations.

Nowadays, the world television community is serviced by three standards: NTSC, SECAM (Systéme Electronique Couleur Avec Memoire, used in France) and PAL, with the latter providing the most effective process for maintaining compatibility between monochrome and colour. Although it is not worth pursuing to any substantial technical level the encoding mechanism employed by the three systems, it is, however, worth noting that the encoding process does destroy some colour information present in the original scene. Designers working with television must be aware of the restrictions colour transmission encoding places on their images. For example, raw primary colours, especially red, are prone to noise, which appears as a 'boiling' effect in the image, and is exacerbated when the images are processed by consumer video recorders.

Another constraint is presented by the 3:4 height-to-width ratio of the television screen. The designer must utilize this screen space or devise layouts which effectively alter the aspect ratio. Although the current aspect ratio is not perceived as any major disadvantage, the proposed high definition TV format of 9:16 will extend the landscape format even more and perhaps create a problem of compatability.

Another feature of television technology is the sampling process introduced by the television camera; any sampling process will introduce aliasing errors (see Glossary) when levels of detail exceed certain system limits. In the case of PAL, an image is compressed into 625 lines, of which only 576 are used for encoding the image; the rest are used to carry other types of data. In the NTSC system only 486 lines are available.

This sampling process is also a warning to designers against using fine detail in their images, as this will provoke moiré fringing (see Glossary) in the television receiver. Artwork should not include fine horizontal lines as these will conflict with the raster sampling process, and small typefaces will also be unreadable if their x-height is only a few rasters high. Digital technology tends to confuse these decisions, as very often a designer views the final images upon a high-quality monitor, which is not how the images are seen by the average viewer. Images are first encoded, amplified and transmitted. Badly oriented aerials intersect these signals, which are then amplified and decoded. There is also a very good chance that they are finally seen upon a defocused, poorly adjusted television set. Only when television images are seen displayed upon monitors can their initial high quality be appreciated.

Although the sampling process causes certain unwanted visual aliasing artefacts, it does provide a convenient mechanism for storing images in a digital form, which leads to an exciting world of image manipulation.

News and current affairs programmes rely heavily upon graphics prepared using paint systems, caption generators and video effects machines. Here we see a graphic designer working in a studio supported entirely by electronic design aids.
Courtesy: BBC Television.

VIDEO EFFECTS

To appreciate the myriad effects a computer can introduce to a television image it is necessary to consider some simple mental experiments. A colour

Top: Digital effects systems provide the graphic designer with a range of image manipulation facilities that are only possible with this technology. This example illustrates the 'page turn' which has become a familiar technique for moving from one scene to another. It is just one of the effects offered by Ampex's ADO 500 system.
Courtesy: Ampex Corporation.

Bottom: This digital effect shows how an apparently solid extrusion of colour can be developed from an animated live video image.
Courtesy: Ampex Corporation.

video image can be represented as three colour separations, which can in turn be stored digitally within a computer's memory. One easy exercise is to repeatedly slide each pixel one position to its left. Those pixels that effectively 'fall off' the image on the left-hand side can be reinserted on the right-hand side. In fact, a simple electronic circuit can produce this horizontal slide, together with a vertical slide, without introducing sophisticated computer processors. However, a computer programmed with suitable software can perform a whole variety of pixel manipulations. For example, all the odd lines can be made to slide to the left, while the even lines slide to the right. A delay could be introduced on each raster, so that the top of the image moves first, followed in time by lower raster lines.

Another type of image manipulation results from exchanging the colour primaries by making the red component of a pixel equal to its blue component, while the blue becomes the green, which in turn becomes the red. This type of pseudo-colouring can either be made electronically or controlled by a computer program which could introduce the effect over a period of time.

These and similar manipulative operations are the basis of video effects machines which play an important role in television graphics. Some effects require very little processing power, such as pixel sliding, but others can demand some sophisticated circuits if image quality is to be preserved. For example, if the size of an image had to be reduced by half, a first solution might be that every other raster could be dropped, and every alternate pixel on the remaining rasters were deleted. Although a recognizable picture would still result, it would be awash with objectionable visual artefacts that could not be tolerated if the images were moving. Another problem with this approach is that it does not provide a mechanism for moving gradually from the full-size image to the half-size view. To achieve this level of control, digital circuits have to be introduced to manage the conversion.

A solution to the problem is not to reject alternate pixels but to allow their colour intensities to have some influence over the sampled pixel. This means that some process must examine these colour values, multiply them by suitable numeric weights and obtain a final value. Performing this at video rates to three or four hundred thousand pixels requires some clever circuits, but today they are commonplace, and very little attention is given to their performance. Such image manipulation is a trivial exercise for computer-based circuits. In fact, any moving video image can be processed to suggest that it is floating in three-dimensional space, and is subjected to the natural laws of perspective.

Ampex have pioneered video effects systems for many years, and their equipment is a standard feature of any modern television control room. Their recent ADO 500 system is capable of creating a wealth of magical effects in real time. For instance, any video image can be seen in perspective and turned like a page in a book to reveal another image. The system can even introduce a second image as the back of the first image is revealed.

A similar effect enables an animated image to be 'flown in' from some distant point to a selected position on the screen, and part of an image can then be selected and swept through space to create extrusions of solid colour.

Another video effect which is easy to create and explain is called pixelation. This effectively reduces the resolution of an image by making the pixels larger. It is achieved by taking rectangular groups of the original image, for example a 2 x 2 group, and computing their average colour to colour the new

larger pixel. The process can be repeated for larger pixel groups until they become screen-size. Unfortunately, the graphic process is so predictable that it must be used sparingly.

The key to mixing images

For a variety of reasons, part of one video image often has to be combined with another. One useful application is in news and current affairs programmes, where an interviewer or newsreader is superimposed upon other animated or still images. Another use is in weather programmes where the forecaster can be superimposed over satellite or computer-generated images of maps. The technique for achieving this is called chroma-keying.

Consider the process of placing a newscaster over a new background. To achieve this some electronic circuitry requires access to both images and must be able to extract the newscaster's body from one image and replace corresponding pixels in the new background. It sounds simple, but as yet there is no way an electronic circuit can automatically identify an arbitrary silhouette within an image. However, with a little help the process can be made automatic.

If the newsreader is placed in front of a plain colour background (blue is a good example, as hardly any blue is found in skin colour), this colour can act

An essential feature of any television facility is the ability to create a real-time composite from two or more video sources. In this example, a newsreader is superimposed upon another background using a technique known as chroma-keying.
Courtesy: Independent Television News.

as a key when the video image is analysed electronically. Consider one raster in the middle of the screen which contains the blue background and one slice of the newscaster's head. When this raster is processed horizontally, the colour blue will be detected during the first part of the scan, followed by flesh tones, which are in turn followed by blue pixels. The system can now identify at which pixel the head begins and ends.

If both the original and substitute background images are scanned synchronously, electronic circuits can be instructed to create a third image using the new background whenever blue is detected in the first image, otherwise it must carry across the newscaster's head to overwrite the new background.

The blue part of the image provides the chrominance-key (hence the name chroma-key) for separating the foreground from the background stored as a separate element. Obviously the image substitution occurs at video rates which enable the newscaster to move about in front of the blue background. Although blue backgrounds were the choice of the original analogue circuits, digital techniques enable a range of chrominance values to be used and provide greater flexibility.

This type of image composition is widely used in television as it is very cost-effective and still enables

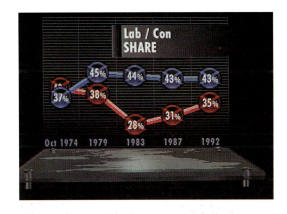

low-budget productions to be visually exciting. Although it was initially introduced as a means for substituting alternate backdrops, some programme makers have experimented with making the foreground characters explore the virtual 3D space painted into a background. This use of chroma-keying is very powerful but requires great skill in balancing the perspective in the background with the optical perspective foreshortening created by the television camera. The eye and brain are very quick to detect the smallest visual inconsistency – even subtle differences in the foreground and background lighting can destroy the illusion.

The live graphics system created for the 1992 British General Election by Matthew Wiessler and Patrick Bedeau took almost two years to prepare and was generated on a Paintbox.

The constant flow of information graphics was used to generate news items throughout the night.
Courtesy: BBC Television.

PAINTING PIXELS

In Chapter 1 we examined the technology of electronic paint systems which can be used for originating completely new digital images. Systems like Quantel's Paintbox provide a perfect environment for performing these operations. Such a system permits any type of artwork to be input via a video camera and stored within the system's memory. This can then be enhanced with a wide variety of tools to achieve a desired effect. But the most important aspect of the technology is the digital nature of the image; no matter how many times it is stored upon

In mid-1990 all 2,400 election candidates were photographed against the same background in three-quarter right profile. Each portrait was stored on the Paintbox, ready to be selected on election night and combined with up-dated results to produce graphics sequences like the exit poll above.
Courtesy: BBC Television.

magnetic disk, retrieved and examined, the quality does not deteriorate. Digital encoding implies zero image degradation.

Even though digital images demand relatively large amounts of disk storage, paint systems are equipped with Gbytes of disk storage for maintaining large image libraries. This enables a graphic designer to quickly prepare a piece of artwork electronically by first browsing through the digital library to identify a map, logo or political figure. Perhaps even incorporate a recent image from video, annotate it with suitable text and within minutes create an image that can be released into the broadcast system during a live news programme. The annotating text can either be introduced by the paint system while the image is being created, or by a separate device called a video character generator. This electronic machine stores many typefaces which can be converted into a video format simply by typing in the required text. This video signal is then combined with the image signal to create an image. No paint, paper, paste or photographs are used – just digital signals.

FLASH HARRY

Historically, graphic designers have always worked with different media, but today's multi-media world dominated by film, video, television and computer graphics enables them to create storyboards that are limited only by their imagination. This new-found visual freedom, where virtually anything can be made to happen, relies upon some very sophisticated editing technology.

Flash Harry is a digital edit suite where any number of image sequences can be input to create one continuous stream of moving images. Its internal digital operation means that there is no image degradation as new effects are introduced, which allows designers to develop highly complex scenes using multi-layering, stencils, dissolves and transparency. Transparency is the key to many effects as it enables one image to be blended with another simply by manipulating the digital pixel codes. However, if the level of transparency is altered in time, one image can be dissolved into another. With the aid of stencils (mattes) and transparency, portions of separate images can be integrated to create complex layers of colour.

Apart from its extraordinary ability to integrate different forms of imagery, Flash Harry includes facilities for electronic painting, retouching, rotoscoping, video effects, perspective, and cel and frame animation. With such an array of features, it is no surprise that Quantel's Flash Harry has had a

Flash Harry's success is derived from its incredible speed and menu-based user interface. This photograph shows the status of the operator's screen during an editing session where input and output image tracks are displayed as columns of numbered frames.
Courtesy: Quantel Ltd.

These two pictures, designed as titles for the Sky Movie Channel, were built up as a series of layers and then manipulated using Quantel's Harriet. This self-contained dynamic graphics workstation combines all the capabilities of the Paintbox with a solid state video store (Ramcorder), video effects and control of an external videotape recorder, producing a single machine capable of very fast production of rotoscoping, retouching, animation and dynamic graphics.
Courtesy: Paul Butler.

These three images are taken from an ITN report on television franchises in the UK. They illustrate the high level of creative design that has become a daily feature of UK television broadcasts. This sequence was created and animated using Quantel's Paintbox and Flash Harry systems.
Courtesy: Independent Television News.

significant influence on graphics for advertising, television and video.

COMPUTER GRAPHICS

Even in the late 1970s, when computer graphics was still relatively young, some graphic designers attempted to use computer-generated images. Unfortunately, the normal method of capturing a computer's design was via the graph plotter, which meant that animation sequences had to be drawn on peg-registered paper or cel.

This was a labour-intensive process, starting with an operator fixing a piece of cel to the computer-driven plotter. When instructed, the computer would trace out its design under the action of a stored program. This might take anything between a few seconds to 15 or 20 minutes; much depended on the complexity of the image, and in particular, whether the computer had to remove hidden lines from a 3D scene. On completion, the operator removed the cel, which was then allowed to dry, and replaced it with another. This cycle was repeated until the animation sequence was complete.

To gauge the time needed for this process, consider a ten-second animation sequence which would have required 250 images (assuming it was

Creating an ident for an international television company requires extraordinary design skills: it must be recognized immediately by the viewing public; it must be in character with the corporate body it represents; and it must be able to withstand a long exposure to public viewing without becoming dated. In these three images taken from an animated sequence, models, Paintbox, Encore and Harry were creatively combined to produce an award-winning sequence for BBC Television. *Courtesy: BBC Television. Designed, directed and produced by Lambie-Nairn & Company Ltd.*

intended for the UK PAL system). If each cel took 10 minutes to draw, the total sequence would have taken 2,500 minutes – just over 40 hours. But this was not the end of the process. The next stage was to film it, and if the designer was not happy with the animated movements, the computer program was modified and a new batch of cels drawn.

Having arrived at an acceptable sequence, the cels were either back-painted (see Glossary), as in traditional animation, or converted to high-contrast negatives which could be used to produce coloured optical lines on a black background.

Nowadays, the process is completely different. The designer passes a storyboard over to a computer animator and discusses the project in detail, for it could be that the images output by the computer will have no further work done on them, and will be broadcast as they stand. These techniques are described in Chapter 7.

Animated television graphics

Animated television graphics are used for programme titles, company idents and logos, trailers, and illustrative graphics, as well as news and business programmes, where an animated sequence communicates much more information than any description could. These sequences are particularly

Ravensbourne College of Design and Communication is prepared to meet the demands of industry, for they have installed one of the most sophisticated video facilities in the academic world. Students have access to professional sound and video systems which include a Quantel Paintbox and Harriet digital edit suite. In an end-of-course examination, student Sarah Rees was given ten days to conceive and produce an idea for the title sequence to head up a pop video programme.

To produce the sequence, Sarah used a combination of video stop-frame animation, live action and Harriet. After experimenting with an EOS animation recorder, live footage and animation was input to Harriet, which was used for rotoscoping and moving the elements around in 3D space. These three images are part of the project. (See also detail on page 90.) *Courtesy: Sarah Rees, Ravensbourne College of Design and Communication.*

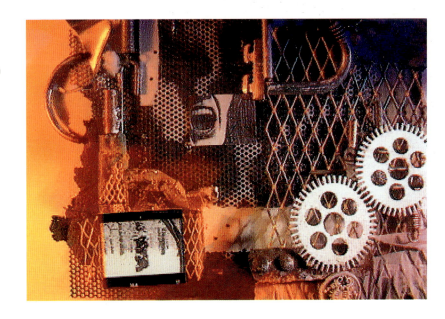

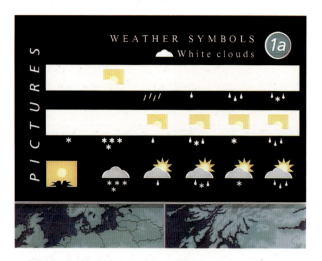

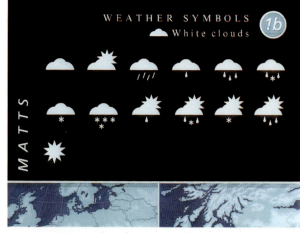

These pictures are from a Sky News weather presentation. The weather symbols, the map and the completed chart were all generated on the Quantel Paintbox. The perspective on the maps themselves was achieved through distortion on an A64 Digital system and embellishments were added on the Paintbox.

The weather symbols are placed daily over the maps using a keying system.
Courtesy: Mike Hurst (British Sky Broadcasting) and Paul Butler.

useful in displaying animated histograms describing, for example, share performance on international stock exchanges, unemployment statistics, and local and national election results.

Again, the flexibility introduced by software means that programs can be written in advance to produce the animation. However, the final heights of the histogram elements, or the points on a graph, can be entered at the very last moment before going on air, which ensures that the data which is eventually broadcast is as accurate and up to date as possible. Frequently, video paint systems such as Quantel's Paintbox are used for this purpose.

Another approach involves using hardware which stores images or information in a compressed format. Prior to broadcasting the programme, the designers prepare their images and sequences using on-line maps, digital picture libraries, and electronically gathered news items. When they are needed, the studio director can request any sequence of images, at which point the hardware decodes the individual images for broadcasting at video rates. Without this initial stage of image compression and preparation, it would be difficult for a computer to create the sophisticated level of realism and detail found in these graphics, which often contain features like reflections and shadows.

CASE STUDY: *AROUND THE WORLD IN 80 DAYS*

Creating a title sequence for a new television programme is always an exciting opportunity for a graphic designer, as they often have considerable artistic freedom in their solutions. In this case study, Liz Friedman's brief was to design the title sequence for the BBC's programme *Around the World in 80 Days* featuring Michael Palin. This series of programmes was to record Michael Palin's journey around the world in his attempt to complete the trip in under 80 days.

Liz Friedman's storyboard reflected the problems of travelling across continents with the ultimate goal of an 80-day deadline. The central graphic elements were a world map, a clock face and a scale of days, upon which were superimposed images of Michael Palin, date stamps, postcards, and historic buildings. The map, clock and scale were combined as rotating concentric features, each having their own speed, while the other images were introduced as overlays, many in an animated form.

Integrating so many graphic elements could only be achieved with the use of digital technology – in this case Quantel's Paintbox, Encore and Harry systems. However, low-tech ideas and subterfuge are still vital to the success of many projects, and also keep the project in budget. For example, to show a rotating Eiffel tower, a model of the tower was shot as it rotated slowly on a turntable. But in order to mask out the background and the turntable, it was shot again using backlighting. This last sequence provided the mattes which would eventually allow the Eiffel tower to be isolated as an individual entity.

The various pieces of artwork were then input through a video camera, while the animated video sequences were converted to a digital format. The Quantel Paintbox provided an environment where

106

last-minute modifications could be made to the artwork, and different graphic elements could be composited. Encore, which is the electronic equivalent to a computer-controlled motion rig, was then used to rotate the day and clock scales together with the world map. At each stage of manipulation the designer was able to experiment with different speeds and configurations and see the effect in real time. A more traditional technique could not have provided such flexibility.

However, when creating multi-layered graphics where individual layers have a complex structure, decisions must be made to accept one layer and proceed with the compositing process. These are valuable skills that graphic designers acquire with their use of digital systems. In this project, Liz Friedman had to make many on-the-spot decisions as Harry was used to develop the delicate semi-transparent layers of animation.

The Harry suite was vital to the final digital composition as it provided a real-time environment for introducing the still and animated overlays. The digital nature of the images ensured that no matter how many times they were composited, the final image would retain the original colours and details.

These three images were taken from the final title sequence from *Around the World in 80 Days.* It is possible to see how the image of the Eiffel Tower has been incorporated within the individual frames. The final compositing was achieved using Quantel's Harry system. *Courtesy: BBC Television and Liz Friedman.*

'No person who is not a great sculptor or painter can be an architect.
If he is not a sculptor or painter, he can only be a builder.'

JOHN RUSKIN

6 Architecture

This image has been rendered completely from a 3D description of the building, with shadows, shading, texture and reflections added by the Wavefront computer graphics system.
Courtesy: Created by Corrigan Loverde in New York using Wavefront Visualizer software and GDS.

Left: A close-up of the structural detail of the front wall of Lambeth Bridge House. This was part of a design study by EPR Architects to explore new methods of construction.
Client: British Land plc.
Courtesy: EPR Architects Ltd.

INTRODUCTION

Architects offer their design skills in a wide variety of areas, from designing a small extension on a private dwelling, to the layout of a new urban development. They are constrained by budgets, timescales, building regulations, fire and safety regulations, environmental restrictions, building materials, and planning committees. Many people would argue that these constraints are necessary, as ultimately we must all live or work within their designs which can have a lifetime measured in hundreds of years. Some designs, however, suffer the humiliation of being razed to the ground long before their natural life-span is over. Mistakes are made, as in any design process, but unlike an advertising poster campaign that goes wrong and can be quickly replaced by another, a building that slips through various planning safety nets is often left as a blot on the landscape. It is ironic, however, that some 'blots' can become 'masterpieces' (for example St Paul's Cathedral), while some 'masterpieces' are destroyed as 'blots'.

As we move towards the twenty-first century, architects will be further constrained by pressure groups pursuing campaigns to preserve our architectural heritage; by an increasing public awareness of the impact architecture has upon social behaviour; and by the problems of sensing how fast society will accept changes towards some of the abstract and 'brutal' characteristics of modern architecture. Never before has there been a time when architects need access to design tools that allow them to create, assess and modify designs until an optimum solution is obtained, which is why many architectural practices have turned to computers to aid them in their difficult task.

EARLY WORK

Architects cannot be criticized for not recognizing the benefits computers have to offer: together with industrial designers they explored the applications of the first 2D CAD systems and quickly discovered that the computer's flexibility in maintaining files of line drawings was relevant to much of their work. Many projects consisted of preparing elevations and plans of buildings; 3D perspectives were not particularly important. Large projects could always be visualized using scale models which, even with today's advanced technology, still play an important role.

These drafting systems offer features such as database management, multi-layered schematics, feature libraries, automatic dimensioning, variable scaling, and annotation. A computerized database enables everything from bricks to window frames to be allocated reference codes; it stores dimensions, suppliers and costs; it is organized hierarchically for rapid retrieval; and is online to the draftsperson whilst drawing.

The multi-layering feature enables certain types of information to be held as separate files: for example, electrical wiring diagrams would be isolated from the water and gas supplies, and the annotation would also be a distinct layer. But even though the layers are separate, it is still possible to display them in any combination with the line drawing. Feature libraries permit elements to be drawn once and referenced any number of times throughout a drawing. For example, whenever a window frame is modified, the library entry is updated and a new drawing requested which automatically includes all of the changes.

Once specific overall dimensions have been allocated to a structure, other internal dimensions can be supplied by the drafting system simply by identifying two points on the drawing. If any subsequent changes are made to the drawing, the drafting software automatically computes the related internal dimensions. Drawings can be scaled by any factor showing all or some of the schematic layers.

Finally, different elements of the drawing can be annotated and repositioned whenever new features are introduced. These are powerful features of any design system and were not available on any manual system – hence the keenness of the architectural profession to explore these early systems.

3D MODELS

In recent years, CAD systems have evolved dramatically, and now offer a variety of 3D modelling and visualization features; these too have been taken on board by architects. The ability to work in three dimensions has not meant abandoning 2D drafting,

These two views of a proposed building capture precisely the scale and proportion of the project. Once the original 3D geometry is input to the CAD system, any number of views can be obtained with hidden lines removed to clarify the images.
Project: Kantoorgebouw Breda Spoor.
Architect: Blom Partners bv Beda.
Computer drawings: Peter Zenger.

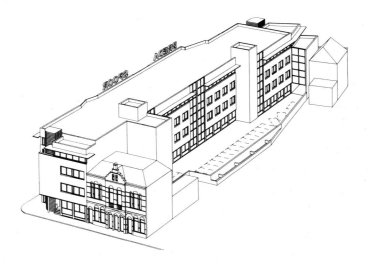

because a large percentage of an architect's work is still two-dimensional. Drawings are not just an intermediate illustration to show to a client, they become reference documents for the final construction of a structure. However, although 3D perspective drawings have their own special uses, they cannot be derived automatically from an arbitrary set of 2D elevations.

Making scale models for a large project can have certain benefits. For example, a group of people can view a model simultaneously; it can be decorated with texture and natural features such as trees; it can be illuminated to show shadow footprints; it can be incorporated with other surrounding buildings; but it can also be expensive. Scale models might not have the flexibility to explore 'what if' scenarios, and they cannot be easily coloured to explore colour schemes.

The main advantage of holding 3D models within a computer arises from the geometric nature of the data. As overall dimensions are maintained, rather than some preferred perspective view, computer graphics techniques enable the data to be processed to reveal any arbitrary view of the model. The ability to place an imaginary camera anywhere within a building cannot be overstated. Never before have architects been able to explore the internal spaces of their structures with the flexibility offered by

computers. Room interiors can be fitted with various alternate furnishings and the 'virtual' camera can explore exactly how it would look in reality. Already, experimental Virtual Reality systems are being used to take real-time journeys through architectural databases and provide designers with a visualization tool they have never possessed. Although such systems are only laboratory projects, they are identifying powerful new design aids for the future.

REALISM

The computer program that creates the coloured image from a 3D database is called a renderer; this can cover surfaces with real-world texture, incorporate realistic backdrops and even introduce artefacts such as trees, cars, fountains, birds and humans. However, many modern buildings employ vast amounts of glass and metal, and when visualizing such structures, reflections and shadows are important features. Ray tracing can be used to reveal shadows and specular reflections, and when used with a large database it can take several hours to compute just one frame. Therefore, animating a walk-through using ray tracing could be time-consuming and expensive.

Another aspect of 3D visualization concerns the impact a large construction project, such as a power station, will have upon the environment. One simple computer-based method is to employ a paint system and overlay a computer-generated image onto a photograph. In order that both image elements share a common perspective, the location, orientation and camera lens data must be used to render the 3D computer model. The obvious drawback with this technique is that it is difficult to develop an animated sequence which might identify weaknesses in the proposed layout.

An alternative approach, which permits the animation of the final scene, involves digitizing a contour map of the required terrain to create a 3D model of the terrain's surface. This can be rendered using texture maps derived from aerial photographs. Finally, the proposed building complex can be integrated with the ground terrain to create a unified database, which can be viewed from any point in space. The animation sequence is created by preparing a 3D trajectory in space along which the computer's virtual camera will travel, and as it makes its journey it captures individual scenes which when recorded on video tape or a laser disk provide the real-time animation when played back.

The two main benefits computers bring to an architect's drawing board are: a flexible system for maintaining two- and three-dimensional geometric information, and a powerful tool for creating rendered views of the final structure. However, the computer does not stop here – it has many other roles to play in providing extra information from the digital data.

VOLUME INTERSECTIONS

One of the problems of designing any complex 3D structure concerns data integrity. Any single element can easily be designed, but knowing that it does not interfere or intersect with other elements is vitally

For this image, taken from the Snowhill, Birmingham project, YRM Partnership Ltd used models built in Intergraph Microstation and rendered in Modelview on Unix workstations.

Shadows were produced by ray tracing and merged with the final image, and reflections were produced by environment mapping from site photographs.

Materials such as stone were captured by colour scanning on Mac Microtech and applied by texture mapping during rendering. The people were selected from a scanned image library and applied to 2-metre-square shapes in design model with a transparent background.
Courtesy: YRM Partnership Ltd.

important. When designing a building, doors must be able to open without obstructing other features such as joists, pillars and staircases. It must be possible to position air ducting in ceiling cavities without intersecting other structures. Similarly, electrical, gas and water services must be easily accessible for installation and future servicing. Computer software is able to undertake such tests and report back where possible intersections exist or where a minimum tolerance is discovered. Even 3D drawings of the offending data clash can be supplied to provide a clear interpretation of what has gone wrong.

AREA, VOLUME AND STRUCTURAL CALCULATIONS

The role of an architect can frequently appear daunting. A structure must be designed that will support its own weight, and it must provide an efficient ratio of useable space related to total volume. It must not employ expensive building materials that force it to run over budget, but at the same time it should be aesthetically pleasing to the people who will inhabit its interior and share its exterior. While balancing these various parameters, the architect simultaneously strives to introduce a personal expression of shape, form and space into the equation, without incurring the wrath of the frustrated architectural talent many bystanders claim to possess.

To help resolve this quandary, the computer can offer extra design aids in the form of computational tasks. For example, floor areas and wall surfaces can be calculated from architectural databases and related to the total structural volume. Room volumes can be derived which may be useful in heating calculations and determining the air-conditioning plant to achieve minimum cycles of air changes.

Maximum floor loadings can be computed, and load-bearing walls checked to ensure statutory building regulations are met. Using techniques such as Finite Element Analysis, 3D structures can be investigated to determine the stresses and strains they would suffer if unusual loads were applied. Stress simulation is vital to developing the special foundations needed to support buildings located on terrain with a history of earthquakes.

LIGHTING AND ILLUMINATION LEVELS

The orientation of a building has a significant impact on internal illumination levels, shadow volumes and temperature levels. Surrounding buildings will also influence the choices available to an architect and will have to be modelled together with the proposed building when the computer is involved in simulating illumination levels.

To evaluate such scenarios, the relevant 3D portions of the environment are input to a computer program which, given the relative position of the sun, can perform illumination calculations at any time of the day. For instance, a series of images can be created to show shadows caused by surrounding buildings. Contour maps of illumination levels can be

The combination of a Personal Computer and a modern CAD package is a cost-effective environment for supporting project management tasks in interior design and architectural applications. In this example, a desktop CAD system was used to develop the 2D plan of an exhibition stand. The flexibility of the computer model allowed the designer to explore a wide variety of scenarios with the client and quickly develop an optimum solution. The final layout was then used to provide accurate drawings for the exhibition stand contractor for identifying the dimensions and positions of free-standing screens, desks, seats, and decorative plants, together with electrical wiring diagrams locating sockets and switches. The photograph illustrates the completed exhibition stand. *Courtesy: Imagination Ltd and British Telecom.*

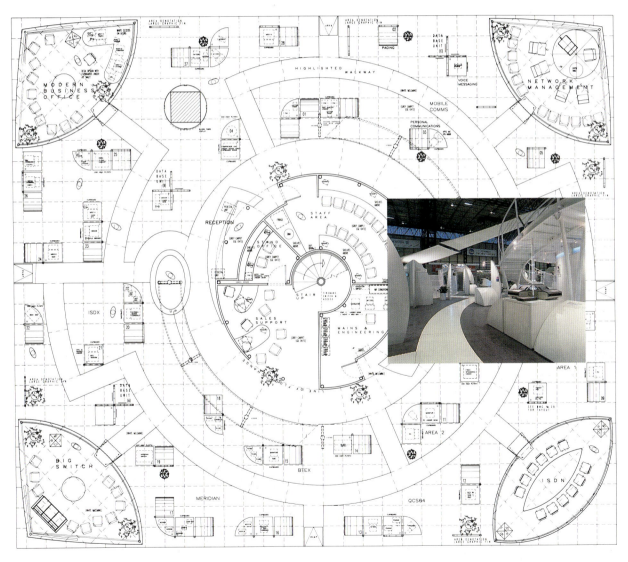

Protecting the Sphinx and the
Gizeh Pyramid is not an easy
task, and in this proposed
solution we see a visualization
created by the application of
3D computer graphics and a
paint system. The roof
structure was first modelled
using the Softimage 3D
computer graphics system and
then composited, by Seb
Janick, with an original
photograph on Quantel's
Graphic Paintbox.
*Courtesy: Pascal Herold,
DUPON.*

computed for different floors, and internal areas of shadow can be derived as the sun's relative position changes during the day. Such calculations can be made at any time of the day and year, and could even be shown as an animated sequence.

From this preliminary data it is possible to consider strategies for placing other sources of illumination. However, the illumination levels of interiors are very sensitive to the juxtaposition of walls, lights and windows, which generate complex sequences of reflections. Fortunately, radiosity, which has always been used by architects, enables these diffuse multi-reflections to be computed, but the technique is mathematical and involves solving many equations. Nevertheless, with the assistance of computer software, very complex interiors can be simulated and provide very realistic images.

Until recently, radiosity calculations needed large computers and long periods of time to render one image; but with the use of incremental radiosity and multi-processors, it will soon be possible to perform these simulations in real time.

NEW STRUCTURES

It has been said that 'Architecture mirrors society; its civility and its barbarism.' And it is also true that architects must recognize social trends and respond by providing the buildings that support and reflect such group behaviour. The very way we shop today has serious implications for the fate of the friendly high-street store and the design of future shopping precincts. Supermarkets and hypermarkets demand large structures that provide the greatest flexibility in floor layouts.

Modern materials and cantilevered structures have finally released architects from the straightjacket that building principles handed down over the centuries

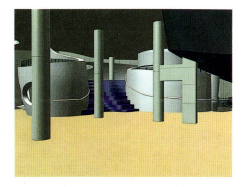

This staircase is part of the foyer designed by Ron Arad Associates for the Tel Aviv Opera House. The model was created using EMS – Engineering Modelling System (Intergraph) – at McColl by Caroline Brown.
Courtesy: Ron Arad Associates Limited.

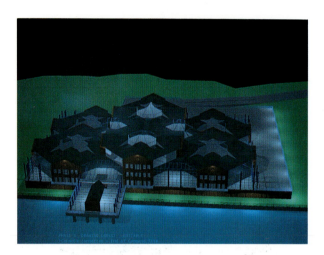

Thirty six light sources were used to illuminate this computer model of the new headquarters for the Colonial Mutual Group at Chatham Dock Yard. The building was modelled and rendered using GDS.
Client: Colonial Mutual Insurance Ltd.
Architect: EPR Architects Ltd.

have created. Externally supported walls and roofs have provided a totally new approach to building design. These are exciting concepts and are readily evaluated for structural soundness and aesthetics within the privacy of a computer's memory.

Computers provide a complete three-dimensional work environment within which the architect can design, visualize, and evaluate new building projects. Moreover, they play a valuable part in the day-to-day organization of an office including multi-media client presentations, spreadsheet analyses, data capture, corporate reports, and project costings. Their role is no longer seen as a peripheral activity, but a central integrating force.

CASE STUDY: CAD IN ARCHITECTURE

EPR is a successful architectural practice, based in central London, where CAD plays a central role in all of their design work. It is used for preparing initial design studies, together with detailed visualizations of exterior elevations, roof structures, atria, interior perspectives, shadow footprints and evaluating artificial lighting scenarios.

The CAD system is GDS which is marketed by Electronic Data Systems. This provides facilities for modelling very complex 3D structures which can be displayed as line drawings with hidden-line removal, or rendered in colour with multiple light sources and shadows. For example, in the design for a new headquarters for Colonial Mutual Insurance at Chatham dock yard, 36 light sources were used to illuminate the building, which provided their client with an accurate and valuable image of the completed building.

Although the potential of CAD is never underestimated, it is only employed where it offers obvious benefits over other techniques. For example, when a client requires a quick visualization of a proposed building in its future location, it might not be economically viable to model the building and its surrounding landmarks in 3D. These landscapes are often very detailed, perhaps involving bridges, monuments, roads, office blocks and so on, and when the client is only looking for some means of assessing the building's visual impact upon a skyline, CAD must be used sparingly.

One must never loose sight of simple solutions that might only require a camera, tracing paper, pencil and a computer illustration. A quick and effective solution necessitates taking a photograph from some useful elevation, from which various features can be traced and incorporated into a computer-generated line drawing. The final scene can even be decorated with hand-drawn trees to enhance the visual's graphic content. Such a technique is often used by EPR. Only when a client transforms a convincing design study into a commissioned project does CAD begin to play a major role in creating accurate site drawings, annotated plans, exterior elevations, interior perspectives and rendered visuals. One of the first problems relates to capturing accurate dimensions of the proposed site, and only when these dimensions are available can any serious

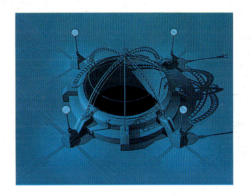

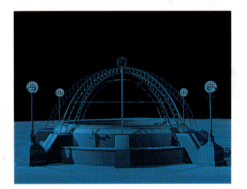

These two views of an atrium feature in the Prudential Assurance Co Headquarters (Holborn Bars) confirm the importance of multiple light sources and shadows in design study visualizations. The structure was modelled using GDS and rendered using its complementary software.
Client: Prudential Portfolio Managers Ltd.
Architect: EPR Architects Ltd.

Apart from providing extraordinary visualizations for design studies, CAD systems have made possible the design of totally new methods of construction. In this design study for British Land plc, EPR explored the use of self-supporting structures for the front wall of Lambeth Bridge House.
Client: British Land plc.
Architect: EPR Architects Ltd.

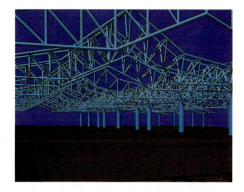

EPR's design solution for London's new fruit and vegetable market at Temple Mills E10 called for a roof structure that provided market traders with work space and minimum interference from supporting walls and columns. *Client: Spitalfield's Development Group. Architect: EPR Architects Ltd.*

work begin in mapping out features of the building.

One reason why CAD is so successful in architectural applications is that buildings often contain structural or decorative features that are employed many times; this means that they need only be modelled once and duplicated any number of times. Such modelling techniques were used by EPR in the roof structure for London's Spitalfield Development Group fruit and vegetable market.

Nowadays, architects have access to a wide range of building materials and construction techniques that make it possible to explore more advanced technical designs. CAD techniques are useful because they allow such designs to be mechanically evaluated and visualized in software. EPR's design study for Lambeth Bridge House is typical of the sophisticated structures that are a feature of their projects.

EPR's experience in working on large architectural projects has created challenging opportunities for applying their knowledge of CAD, and even though they still utilize scale models for some applications, the computer has become a vital design tool.

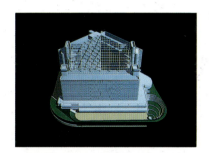

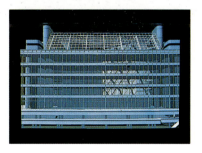

These two views of the new UK headquarters for Sun Life of Canada in Basingstoke, reveal the level of detail and high-quality imaging that have become the hallmark of modern CAD systems. *Client: Sun Life of Canada Ltd. Architect: EPR Architects Ltd.*

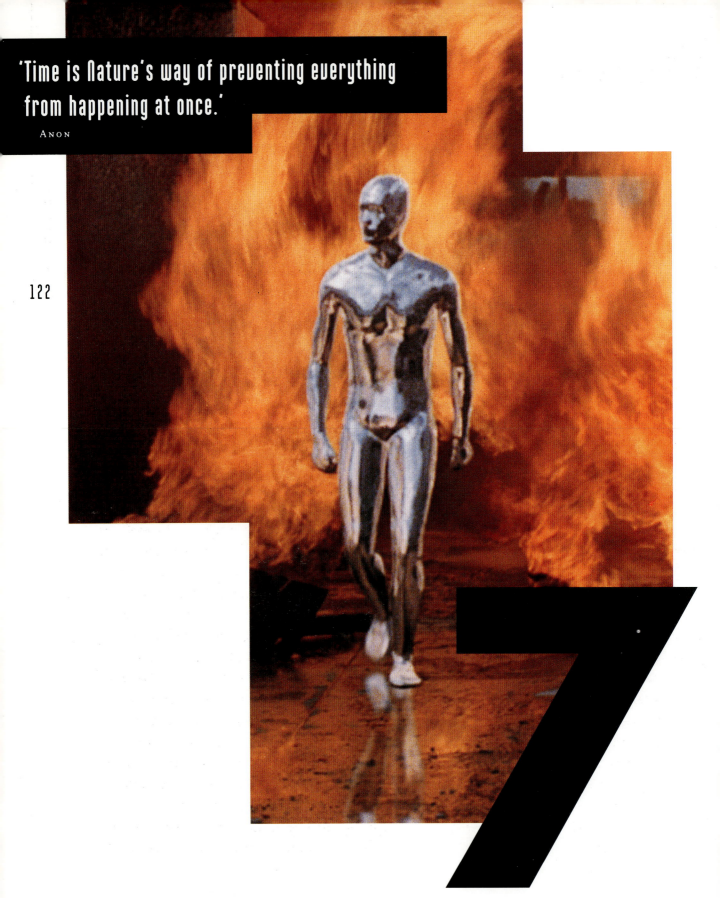

'Time is Nature's way of preventing everything from happening at once.'
ANON

122

7 Animation

THE COMPUTER AS ANIMATOR

When we observe anything moving it appears continuous and free from flicker; the human visual system is able to sample the outside world and form a coherent and continuous visual experience. However, animation works by projecting a sequence of separate images at a refresh rate such that the eye perceives an uninterrupted visual continuum. Both the media of film and television exploit this effect: film projection uses a frame rate of 24 frames/second, whilst PAL television employs 25 frames/second, and NTSC uses 30 frames/second. However, when projecting film, every frame is further interrupted by a shutter to increase the refresh rate to 48 or 72 frames/second. In television each frame is split into two fields which are refreshed at 50 and 60 fields/second for PAL and NTSC respectively. Even the images on computer screens are created using a refresh rate of about 60 frames/second.

Computers are a valuable aid in creating animation effects, as they are able to store different styles of images, retrieve them from memory stores and display them rapidly. Although computers are being employed by the traditional cartoon industry, perhaps their greatest influence has been in their ability to integrate different sources of imagery into an animated sequence.

Animation, as an art form, does not impose any rules or restrictions as to what materials can be used to source the original images. Animators use line drawings on paper, back-painted cel, scale models, modelling clay, and articulated paper models to create their moving images. Some early animators even drew directly onto the film stock. Computers, therefore, are not seen as any real threat to traditional procedures. If they can offer something new to the animator's toolkit then they will survive and be used, otherwise the world of animation will continue to flourish and explore new and exciting methods for animating images.

Fortunately, the computer has much to offer the animation industry and has already had a major influence upon the style and complexity of images we accept and expect on everyday television. When we see, for example, an advertisement for a new car, which appears very real but is squashed, stretched and twisted as it is driven along a road, we don't question the animation technique; in a relatively short period of exposure to computer-processed images we have come to accept images for what they communicate in the form of information, pleasure and excitement. Questions are not asked as to whether they are real or synthetic; whether a car actually exists or is nothing more than a computer program.

Computers are revealing new ways of creating images, and are providing original and creative methods for their processing. But perhaps their most exciting contribution is in 3D applications where computer animation is being used in education, TV, video games, industrial simulation, advertising, scientific visualization, medicine, and film production.

In education, computer animation is frequently used to illustrate geometric, mathematical and scientific principles. Equations and physical laws can be easily translated into two- and three-dimensional animations that provide students with an alternative visual insight into the world of mathematical symbols.

The television industry has been using computer animation for several years. Programme titles, special effects, news and current affairs programmes rely on computers to provide interesting, cost-effective, and flexible methods for creating synthetic images.

Video games have now become very sophisticated and demand a high level of user attention and interaction. Many games take the form of simulation exercises where the player is allowed to drive a racing car or motor bike at dangerous speeds, or even fly a plane and take part in an imaginary air battle. This form of animation is rapidly moving into the domain of Virtual Reality systems where the player is visually isolated from the real world and placed within a virtual synthetic world. Wearing an interactive suit and gloves the player is able to interact with objects that have no physical existence.

Many industries are already using computers for CAD, and can design anything from a bracket to an automobile body. One of the benefits of holding such objects in a digital form is that they can be incorporated into computer programs that subject them to imaginary forces and torques. For example, a car's suspension can be investigated using computer animation techniques; given a suitable graphics workstation, a designer can observe in real time the motion characteristics of a vehicle as it is driven over simulated road surfaces. By interactively changing the parameters controlling the features of the car's suspension, the designer can use animation to identify optimum conditions.

The advertising industry is a major employer of computer animation. Everyday objects such as boxes of soap powder, cans of beer, bottles of bath cleaner, and teapots are digitized in order to create a photo-realistic synthetic image. Then, with the aid of 3D

animation programs, the objects can be made to perform acrobatic tasks that would be impossible with their real-world counterparts. So realistic are these renderings that it is virtually impossible to detect what is real and what is computer-generated.

The domain of scientific visualization depends considerably upon animation techniques to assist in revealing information that is often hidden within large sets of data. In the field of remote sensing, where satellites monitor the world's surface and transmit back to earth vast amounts of data, stereoscopic images enable the 3D surface topology to be computed. Once this geometry has been extracted it is possible, using computer animation, to 'fly' over this terrain. There are now animations which simulate flying over the surface of the Moon and Mars.

Computer animation is finding many applications within medicine. One example is found in the diagnosis of heart conditions which can be assisted with the data obtained from CT scanners. The data slices obtained from such machines can be input to computer programs which are capable of extracting various objects or isolating different layers of tissue. If the heart data are retrieved over different periods of time, the heart can be animated to reveal whether anything abnormal occurs while it is beating.

Finally, in this brief summary of applications,

computer animation is being increasingly used in film making where it can be used for special effects, an alternative to scale models, or simply a unique method for rendering 3D animated scenes. The computer graphics industry even has its own animated film festivals, where animators and researchers share new methods for modelling, rendering or animating. However, unlike traditional cartoon animators who simply draw what they want, a computer has to be programmed at every stage of the animation process. This introduces new and unusual procedures which can be integrated with familiar manual processes to create totally new animations. In order to appreciate the similarity between computer animation and traditional cartoon animation, it is important to review the stages for creating conventional hand-drawn cartoons and then investigate how computers can be used to provide alternative methods.

CARTOON ANIMATION

In the world of cartoon animation, Walt Disney has probably had more influence than any other person, and has left behind a legacy of extraordinary films such as *Snow White and Pinocchio,* and characters like Mickey Mouse. In recent years, films like *Who*

Top: This single frame from an animated sequence for the BBC *Nine O'Clock News* incorporates ideas of incoming data in the form of signals, messages and images. The sequence employs 3D computer graphics to animate the concentric rings, over which are composited multi-layered icons and images. *Courtesy: BBC Television. Designed, directed and produced by: Lambie-Nairn & Company Ltd.*

Bottom: This image is taken from a sequence where computer-animated feathers are used to overlay a transparency transition as a new image is revealed. Alias was used for the computer animation and Harry for the digital editing. *Client: Johnson & Johnson. Agency: Y & R. Animation and Post Production: The Moving Picture Company.*

The Computer Film Company is one of the few companies in the world specializing in digital manipulation techniques for creating special effects in live-action sequences. Frequently, these projects call for the integration of cartoon characters with live action to create a seamless 3D composite.

Although this process is not new, being able to create a convincing effect is, and requires the support of digital technology and some very special software.

Framed Roger Rabbit? have also demonstrated that multi-media techniques, where real images are integrated with synthetic drawings, open up new vistas for exploring imaginary scenarios.

Cartoon animation, however, involves several processes, some being very tedious and costly. The original script is first turned into a storyboard where the plot is expanded into a series of drawings which become the first visual interpretation for assessing any shortcomings in the story. From the storyboard, a soundtrack is produced which is used by the animators to control the movement of their characters. Perfect synchronization between sound and images is vital to animation – without it any belief in the illusion is dispelled. To assist the animator in maintaining synchronization, bar sheets are prepared to describe the individual phonetic sounds and their frame numbers.

Before the animators begin drawing the individual frames, a film, complete with soundtrack, is made from the storyboard images. This is known as an animatic or Leica reel, and provides the director with a first impression of the animated story. Any weaknesses in the plot, staging and soundtrack must be discovered at this stage and corrected – any later corrections are likely to be very expensive.

A team of animators now expands the animatic into the discrete images that will provide the final continuous movement. One technique used for speeding up this process is to use skilled animators to draw vital key frames in a scene while assistants (known as inbetweeners) develop the inbetween frames. Inbetweeners must have clear directions concerning the motion of characters during the key frames. Frequently, elements of a scene are accelerating or decelerating and need to be moved accordingly to create slow-in and slow-out movements.

These images – taken from a commercial for FANTA – demonstrate the precision with which the integration can be achieved. The process involves optical scanning hardware developed by CFC which converts the original 35 mm film to a digital format. The cartoon animation sequences are created using traditional techniques, and are also scanned in to the same format. The digital nature of the images means that they can be subjected to a variety of processes especially for the accurate control of colour balance, which is so important to this technique. Furthermore, other vital visual cues such as shadows, shading, reflections, highlights, motion blur, and splashes can also be introduced with the use of digital painting.

The high resolution of the digital files means that the compositing process does not introduce any aliasing artefacts, which is so important when the images are output to 35 mm cine film and projected in cinemas.
Courtesy: FANTA (Character animation by Passion Pictures) and The Computer Film Company Ltd.

128

This 30-second commercial for the Post Office is based on the illustrative style of British artist Beryl Cook. At first glance it appears to be a traditionally-animated commercial. The reality, however, involved multiple layering and complex post-production.

To achieve a fully rendered finish, the animation had to be done on frosted cels which, being semi-opaque, could not be filmed on top of each other in the normal way. By shooting each character separately (and with a matte pass) Harry was able to layer the animation, thus solving the frosted cel problem.

Also, by isolating the many comic incidents taking place in the background, Jerry Hibbert (the director), was able to exercise greater control over the timing, to maximum effect.
'Fence' for Post Office Counters Ltd.
Agency: GGT.
Courtesy: Hibbert Ralph Animation Ltd.

After line-testing the scenes, the images are cleaned up by artists to create a consistent line quality. The drawings are then traced onto transparent plastic cel and back-painted (see Glossary). Several layers of cel may be used to isolate individual foreground characters which can then be overlaid onto different backgrounds. Finally, the 'sandwich' of cels is lit and photographed. Twenty-four frames are needed for every second of film eventually projected, which means that a 10-minute film requires 14,400 frames. The above processes are well defined and involve many people who manipulate hundreds of thousands of drawings.

The animation industry is not likely to abandon these processes overnight as they are understood and they work. However, the industry is investigating computer technology in an attempt to remove some of the tedium from their work and improve throughput. Computer-controlled line-testing devices already exist where line drawings can be input to a computer's memory and played back in real time. Such systems are very useful for evaluating character movements and determining the spacing of the inbetween frames.

Paint systems with appropriate software are being used for the colouring stage. The line drawing is first captured via a video camera and cleaned up using image processing software. The operator can then develop a palette of colours that will be used to paint the images. After selecting a colour, an interactive stylus is used to identify the zone on the image requiring colouring, and the computer floods this area virtually instantaneously. Great care is needed to ensure that the zone is bounded by a continuous line of pixels, otherwise the colour can 'bleed' into surrounding areas. When this happens, an 'UNDO' command is invoked to restore the image prior to the operation. The operator searches and mends the break in the boundary and continues painting. The final scene can be digitally composited with other images and backgrounds using anti-aliasing software to form a soft transition between one shape and another, and then stored on disk. Eventually, the images can be animated using a laser disk or a conventional video disk and then transferred to video tape for final broadcast.

There are no rules concerning what is possible and what is impossible. If images can be input into a computer, then they can be composited in any manner to achieve an effect. For example, there is no reason why animated puppets should not be photographed against a coloured background and input into a paint system. Chroma-keying (see Glossary) can be used to create the matte to isolate the puppet's shape which is then digitally composited with a synthetic background. This not only relieves the animator from building expensive 3D sets, but provides a new animation style.

Although paint systems provide a unique method for creating and integrating various sources of imagery, they are, however, dependent upon the artistic skills of the operator to render the image. If software plays a more important role in these processes the computer can be used to assist in the rendering and even control the animation of 3D

This 40-second commercial entitled 'Whole lotta Quakin'' utilizes digital technology to the full. Hibbert Ralph produced hand-drawn artwork, along with the shadows and highlights for the steam character, which were then digitized into Harry. The artwork, (solid black shapes on a white background) bore little resemblance to the final screen images, having been put through multiple passes on Harry, building up layers to the right density or transparency for the simulation of real steam.
'Whole lotta Quakin'' for Quaker Oats Ltd.
Agency: BMP/DDB Needham.
Courtesy: Hibbert Ralph Animation Ltd.

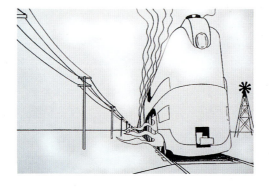

In this project called 'Portside Out, Starboard Home – A Sentimental Journey', the animator wanted to explore the use of electronic airbrushing in a short animation sequence. From an original storyboard, the animator created an animatic where approximate timings were given to each storyboard frame. This was the basis of the line drawing animation which was based on computer-generated images and rotoscoped images. The latter involved the tracing of images onto paper using a 16 mm rostrum film camera. This collection of images was then traced onto white paper in black pencil, adding all the necessary line detail.

The next phase consisted of frame-grabbing the individual drawings into a Quantel Paintbox where they were airbrushed. Paintbox provided facilities to create painted backgrounds and other static elements upon which moving features could be added using stencils.

sequences. To see how different kinds of effects are implemented it is necessary to examine how computers undertake simple animations and then proceed to more complex examples.

Moving Colour

Perhaps one of the simplest forms of animated images is that of colour animation. This uses colour cycles to create an effect of movement by changing the colours of different portions of an image. Consider the shape shown on page 132. This could be interpreted as a cross-section of a pipe which has been coloured with three colours C_1, C_2 and C_3. If this image is stored inside a computer, then the groups of pixels representing the various colours will store numbers referencing the colours being held within a colour look-up table. For example, pixels having a value of 1 will reference the first entry in the look-up table which is C_1, while pixels having a value of 2 will reference the second entry in the look-up table which is C_2. If the colours C_1, C_2 and C_3 are translated as red, green and blue respectively, then the cross-section would be displayed with these particular colour bands.

If the colour look-up table is modified by moving the colours downwards such that the second entry becomes C_1, the third entry becomes C_2, and the first entry C_3, the image on the screen will change. In fact, those pixels having a value of 1 will now become blue; pixels having a value of 2 become red, while pixels having a value of 3 become green. The colours have all appeared to step along one band of the original image. If this process is continuously repeated under the control of a computer program the effect of animated movement can be created without anything really moving. Obviously this has limitations in the ways it can be applied, but nevertheless, it is effective and simple to implement.

The final phase involved editing the images into a coherent sequence with dissolves, cuts and special effects, and also adding the soundtrack. This was all accomplished on Quantel's Flash Harry edit system and then output to broadcast quality video tape.
Courtesy: Paul Norris, Bournemouth and Poole College of Art & Design.

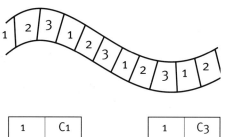

1	C1
2	C2
3	C3

LUT

1	C3
2	C1
3	C2

LUT

A simple method of creating animated movement, where bands of colour appear to move, exploits the use of look-up tables. The shape containing the colour bands is assigned numeric values which reference the colours inside a look-up table (LUT). However, if these colour descriptions are cycled within the LUT, the original bands will appear to move in sympathy.

Shape inbetweening

Assistants are used to expand the key frames drawn by animators to create the inbetween frames and great care is needed in drawing the inbetweens as their relative positions control the animated speed between the key shapes. Inbetweening can be achieved through shape interpolation, which is also used in digital typography for developing families of fonts related to two or more reference fonts. For two-dimensional shape inbetweening, two key shapes are prepared. However, as shapes are held as lists of coordinates, one cannot just find intermediate lists of coordinates interpolated from the reference values, for the animator is interested in keeping portions of one shape to evolve into corresponding parts of another. To achieve this the animator must identify important points on the first shape and where they should be located on the second shape; with this information, computer software can easily develop the inbetween shapes.

A convenient technique that satisfies both shape definition and shape inbetweening is that of Bézier curves. We saw in Chapter 3 that Bézier curves are used for defining the form of outline typefaces, and by adjusting the positions of the control points, portions of the curve can be shaped. Therefore, if the same Bézier technique is used for describing shapes of cartoon characters, then the character can be adjusted to another position by moving its control points. The inbetweening is then effected by interpolating the control points, which are then used to develop the associated curved outline.

The next stage is to control the speed of the inbetweening. Again, this is a simple task for software but guidance is needed from the animator. Several mechanisms exist to communicate this to an animation system but perhaps the simplest to understand is expressed in the form of a curve. The

These three curves can be used to control the degree of interpolation associated with an inbetweening process. The first curve describes a linear amount of inbetweening with the frame count; the second curve shows an accelerated relationship; while the third curve describes a sequence faired at both ends.

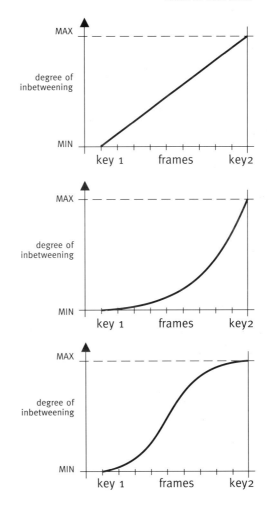

illustration on the right (top) shows a straight-line graph relating the degree of inbetweening and the associated frame number. At frame KEY1 there is minimum inbetweening, therefore the computer draws the first key frame. At frame KEY2 there is maximum inbetweening, therefore the computer draws the second key frame. At intermediate frames the computer draws inbetween frames that are positioned at equal times between the two extremes and consequently create a constant animated speed.

The next illustration shows a curve relating the degree of inbetweening to the frame numbers. Because a curve is used, rather than a line, the amount of inbetweening initially changes very slowly and becomes increasingly larger until the final key frame is reached. This results in a slow-out movement followed by an acceleration. The third curve shows how a slow-out followed by a slow-in movement is obtained. Similar graphical techniques can be used to link several key frames together and thereby provide the animator with greater control over complex movements.

3D COMPUTER ANIMATION

The traditional world of animation is neither 2D nor truly 3D – it is somewhere between the two. Although it is easy for an animator to draw a single picture in perspective, it is extremely difficult to create an animated sequence where the viewer is rotating in this world. This is why many animations rely on movements that are achieved through pans and zooms. Further visual interest is introduced by cutting from one view to another, but rarely does one see a continuous move of the camera from two totally different positions.

Rotoscoping – where drawings are traced from real images – is a technique used by animators to impart a more accurate sensation of three-dimensional movement. Paint systems provide a useful way of creating such animations. One frame of the sequence is input to the paint system and the animator draws those lines needed for the final animation. These lines could be drawn using any style of paint mode, colour and texture, and are held within a separate block of memory. When completed, the image is stored on disk and the same process repeated for every other frame. Obviously this can be a time-consuming process, but it can lead to some interesting animations, and it is not always obvious just how they have been created.

It is also very difficult to draw complex 3D objects moving arbitrarily in space, as the perspective foreshortening of edges presents too many problems.

However, this is easily executed by a computer. Once a 3D object has been digitized and input to a computer it can be viewed from any point in space. Furthermore, very advanced rendering software tools are now available for producing full-coloured views of these objects when illuminated by imaginary lights.

Software environments have also been developed that enable any feature of this virtual world of objects, lights and cameras to be animated. The computer only needs to be told the status of this world at different points in time and, using a similar technique to traditional inbetweening, can compute the inbetween 3D images.

In recent years great strides have been made in making synthetic objects behave the way they do in the real world. For example, a ball can be made to bounce by using the equations of motion to animate its movement. A flag can be animated by simulating the forces that act upon its surface when blown by a breeze, and articulated human characters can be made to walk, run, jump and even talk, with realistic human gestures.

3D modelling

When a 3D model is stored within a computer it is held as a collection of numbers, very often Cartesian coordinates, which fix the position of various features of the object within an imaginary 3D space called 'world space'. For example, a straight line requires six numbers: an x-, y- and z-coordinate for both ends of the line. A rectangle would require twelve numbers: an x-, y- and z-coordinate for the four corners. A cube obviously requires more numbers as it has more vertices (corners), and other 3D objects may require hundreds of thousands of numbers. Fortunately the computer is not intimidated by such quantities – numbers are the stuff of its world, and computers have been designed to process vast quantities of numbers at incredible speed.

However, not all objects are covered in corners that can be assigned three coordinates. Many objects are smooth and continuous such as an apple, a car body or a human face. The input of such objects is sometimes a problem, but a simple subterfuge is to assume that they are covered by a mesh of small polygons, and if this mesh is fine enough it will not be too obvious when displayed on a computer screen. However, if the silhouette of a computer-generated object is examined, this structure is often noticeable in the form of straight edges.

Constructing computer models from flat facets is very common, as modelling procedures such as surface extruding and contour sweeping can be used to build a wide range of useful structures. Extruding is a manufacturing process whereby a material such as plastic or aluminium is forced under pressure through a die. The die's shape then determines the cross-section of the extrusion. This same technique can be implemented in software where an outline 2D shape is used to develop a 3D extruded volume of a given length. It is often used for modelling extruded letters and artefacts such as boxes and cylinders.

Another manufacturing process involves forming a surface as it turns on a lathe. In computer graphics the equivalent modelling technique is used to develop 'swept surfaces' or 'surfaces of revolution'. To construct symmetrical objects such as glasses, spheres, bottles, etc, all that is required is a contour, which when rotated 360 degrees in discrete angles, sweeps out the required surface.

In the world of typography, Bézier curves are used to describe smooth curves for designing fonts. These only require a few numbers, yet can describe smooth curves in two- and three-dimensional space. An extension of this technique allows a few control points in space to define an equally smooth 3D surface patch – these are called Bézier patches. For example, given a matrix of 3 x 3 points in space, a surface patch can be created which touches the four corner points and is pushed and pulled by the remaining five control points. In fact, the technique also extends to a 4 x 4 matrix where the extra control points permit the description of more curved features. Originally, Bézier used collections of these patches to describe the shape of car bodies, but today they have become a useful modelling tool for constructing free-form surfaces as found on telephones, shoes, teapots and furniture.

Rendering

Once an object has been modelled it resides within the computer as a collection of numbers; the next

The asymmetry of this mug means that two modelling techniques are needed to form its surface. The body of the mug employs a sweeping technique where a half cross-section of its body is rotated about a central vertical axis. The handle is constructed by extruding the curved shape through a distance equivalent to its thickness. The two sets of polygons are combined with the handle suitably positioned. *Courtesy: Electric Image Ltd.*

stage is to view it upon a display screen. One simple technique is to display the mesh of lines that form the facets or surface patches. This is called a wireframe view as it appears as though the model is constructed from wire. The ideal requirement, however, is a view where the surface is coloured in and perhaps reveals illumination highlights and shadows – this is known as rendering.

To obtain a rendered image four pieces of information are required: first, an object must be defined and located somewhere within the imaginary world space. Second, the object must be assigned a colour; this might be in the form of levels of red, green and blue, or values of hue, saturation and lightness. Third, the computer needs to know where an imaginary camera is located in world space, and its focal point: this determines how the object will appear on the display screen. Finally, one or more imaginary light sources must be located in world space so that the rendering program can compute the brightness of different parts of the object's surface. Light sources need a location, colour and brightness; if they behave as spot lights, a direction and cone of illumination are also required. Armed with this information the renderer is able to compute the colour intensities of each pixel of a display screen, which might be in the order of one million pixels.

This will take some time and could vary between a fraction of a second to several minutes – much depends upon the complexity of the scene.

Realism

Early computer-generated images betrayed their origin as they were made from simple objects rendered with a handful of colours and contained ragged edges caused by aliasing. Nowadays, researchers have discovered a plethora of techniques for increasing image realism to such an extent that in some circumstances it is impossible to detect its synthetic origin. The maximum number of colours associated with an image is dictated by the number of bits assigned to each pixel. One bit per pixel can store a bi-level image; eight bits per pixel can store 256 grey levels, while eight bits for each primary colour (ie 24 bits) can store 16.7 million colours. Therefore, the number of colours is determined by the number of bits allocated to each pixel in the frame store.

In order to compute the levels of illumination that occur across a surface, the rendering program needs information about the way light is reflected and behaves when it strikes a surface; this is called an illumination model. The more accurate this is, the more realistic the final picture. In 1971 Henri Gouraud developed a model for describing diffuse surfaces, and in 1973 Bui Tuong Phong extended this model to include specular highlights. Both rendering techniques bear their originator's names. Although they are used extensively throughout the computer graphics community they do create images of objects that appear to be covered in plastic.

Realism is greatly improved by covering surfaces with a texture. This is achieved by supplying the renderer with a photograph of a real texture such as wood, marble or cloth, which is then applied to relevant surfaces, taking into account the effects of perspective. Highly polished surfaces do not need any texture as they only reflect their surroundings. These mirror-like reflections can also be simulated by supplying the renderer with images of an environment such as a room, which would probably have four walls, the floor and the ceiling, which can be mapped onto polished surfaces depending upon the orientation of the object and the position of the observer. This commonly-used technique is known as environment mapping.

Unfortunately, none of the above techniques create natural shadows – these must be calculated by separate procedures or using ray tracing. Ray tracing is responsible for a style of imagery that reveals single and multiple reflections, shadows, and refraction. These images often depict scenarios where everything is perfectly clean; every ray of light bounces off precise smooth surfaces, and polished surfaces reflect their environment. In reality, our view of the world contains a mixture of diffuse reflecting surfaces, soft shadows and subtle specular reflections. These can be computed by another technique called radiosity. In fact, radiosity normally only computes the illumination levels arising from multiple diffuse surfaces, but it can also be extended to compute specular highlights.

These three mugs were rendered from the same 3D geometry as the mug on page 136, but using different rendering techniques. The first employs a diffuse shading model, the second introduces specular highlights and the third uses a bumpy texture.
Courtesy: Electric Image Ltd.

Other effects for improving image realism include bump-mapping, 3D texture, particle systems, glows, and atmospheric absorption. Bump-mapping, as the name suggests, is used to cover an object with a simulated bumpy surface such as leather or even orange peel. 3D texture is a technique where various realistic textures such as marble, wood and stone can be described by a computer program. Because the texture description relates to a 3D volume of space, the final model really looks as though it were moulded from the textured material. Particle systems are very large collections of coloured light points, and when a computer program is used to control their colour, position and size they can be used to model a wide variety of special effects. For example, firework explosions are a perfect application for particle systems; a programme simply moves the particles away from some central point with a sudden expansion, and then computes their fall under the action of gravity. Other applications include water spray, forests, corn fields and fire.

Finally, glows and atmospheric absorption are techniques for simulating lighting effects that occur naturally, but have to be deliberately simulated within a computer. However, when the images are animated, no amount of image quality will make up for unrealistic movements.

Modelling natural phenomena
is a particularly difficult
subject; however, in this scene
of Blenheim Palace, the
designer has successfully
captured a sense of scale and
depth. The entire scene is
constructed from several
hundred thousand polygons
and has been rendered with
shadows, atmospheric haze,
and 3D-textured trees.
Courtesy: Gordon Selley,
Coventry Polytechnic and
Rediffusion Simulation Ltd.

ANIMATION

The third component of a computer animation system consists of various techniques for making objects move. In fact, making objects move is relatively easy; making them move realistically is more difficult. Any object can be animated by altering the numbers that describe it within world space (the imaginary reference space within a computer graphics system for storing objects, light sources and the viewing camera). It is also worth noting that, like cartoon animation, computer animated sequences are created one frame at a time. Therefore, a computer animation system needs to be given the starting scenario describing the objects, lights and camera, and then the changes that occur in different parameters for each succeeding frame.

Before each frame is rendered, parameters controlling every object's position in space, rotation, colour and texture are updated. Light sources may be repositioned, and their colour and intensity adjusted. The camera might be repositioned and refocused. When all of these changes have been made, the renderer creates an image based upon the available data. The image is displayed and stored on a medium such as video tape or a video disk which can be played back when all of the images have been computed. If the animation is not to the animator's liking the scene must be rendered again using different parameters.

The secret behind successful animation is knowing how to control the various parameters that determine how objects, light sources and cameras move. Key frame inbetweening is a powerful technique as the parameters only have to be set at specific 'key' frames during a scene; interpolating software is then able to compute the status of the parameters at the inbetween frames. The rules governing the interpolation are best expressed graphically to allow

These three images are part of a metamorphosis sequence between two 3D creatures. To achieve it, the animator used facilities within the CGAL software system to inbetween the 3D geometry of the two creatures, and apply a family of texture maps for each frame. The texture maps were created using a paint facility within CGAL, and provide a rich level of detail to enhance the underlying polygonal structure.
Courtesy: Jacqueline Anne Wrather and Bournemouth Polytechnic.

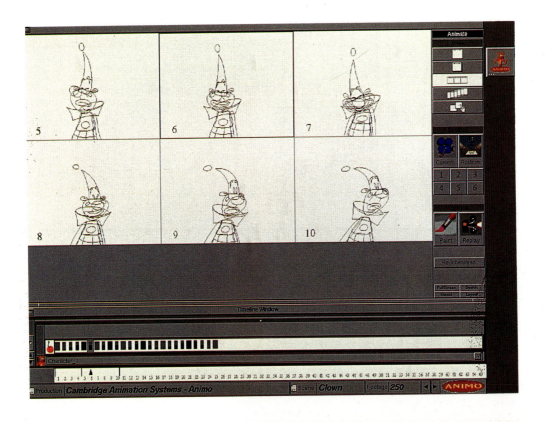

142

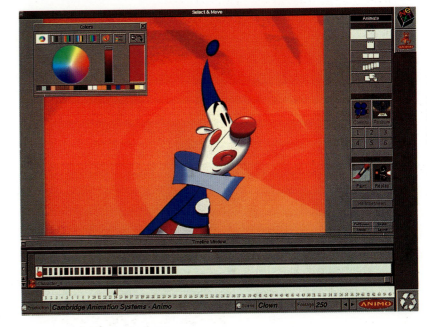

'Animo' is a unique computer animation system that has been designed to address the production problems associated with cartoon animation. The software includes features for inbetweening, real-time line-testing, automatic rendering, camera moves, multi-planes, airbrushing, textures and facilities to output to video and 35 mm cine film. These three images include two views of the interface used by the animator, and an image created using 'Animo'.
Courtesy: Cambridge Animation Systems Ltd.

the animator to control their values at the key frames and the rates at which they are changing. A curve called a spline can then be used to join these key frame parameters to develop values for any intermediate frame.

The above technique works for many applications but in the hands of an inexperienced animator can create a sensation that the animation is over-constrained. Greater levels of realism can be introduced by actually simulating the dynamics of 3D motion and the behaviour of articulated structures. Such approaches rely heavily upon solving sets of mathematical equations relating forces and torques with the accelerations, masses, and moments of inertia for the individual elements of an object. Such simulations are very realistic, and when they are incorporated with the constraints required by the animator, result in some excellent animation. However, animators do not want to become mathematicians; so the interface through which the animator controls the computer must hide all traces of mathematics and allow the animator to communicate with movement and animation.

Animation systems

Most animation houses used to develop their own software to run on mini-computers and graphics

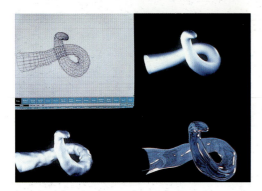

The world of film special effects is dominated by the work of Industrial Light & Magic, who have been responsible for creating stunning computer graphics sequences that have appeared in movies over the past decade. These images from the film *The Abyss* demonstrate how computer animation is used to create effects that would be impossible to achieve without the aid of computer graphics techniques. So effective are the final composites of digital and real images, it is difficult to imagine that the computer-generated images have a numerical origin and are formed from lines and polygons.
The Abyss: © *1989, 20th Century Fox. Courtesy: Industrial Light & Magic.*

workstations. This eventually proved too expensive as programmers were needed to update and maintain the software as new techniques were invented. The modern approach is to use a complete system such as: Alias, CGAL, Explore, Softimage, Symbolics and Wavefront, and enhance these products with in-house programs to resolve any unusual requirements. The benefit of this approach is that the client no longer needs to support a large programming department, and relies upon the software company to update their product as new techniques evolve.

Most systems used by the computer animation industry run on high-performance graphics workstations to benefit from the fast processing speed needed to render the images, which can vary between a few seconds to several minutes. Raw processing speed can make all the difference between the rendering time taking several minutes to an hour.

Apart from the above animation systems, there are many others that are capable of producing excellent animations upon PCs. However, one must always remember that the bottleneck in all computer animation systems is at the rendering stage, which is directly related to the computer's processor speed. Therefore, the selection of the software and the hardware must carefully match the application for which it is intended. All types of computers, from

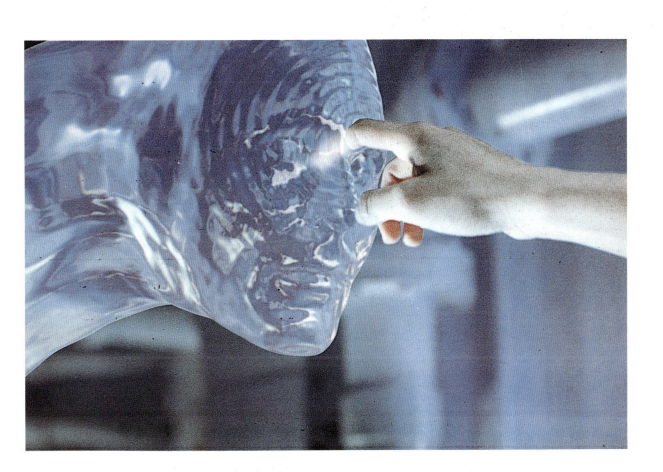

The medium of digital computer graphics provides a world where the laws of physics are suspended, and the impossible happens with such realism, it is difficult not to be convinced. These scenes from *Terminator 2: Judgement Day* cannot convey the tension and drama the animated sequences have in the original film. The menacing qualities of a human-like robot that can take on any solid 3D form would be a challenge for any special effects team, but ILM's mastery of computer graphics and attention to the smallest detail have resulted in computer effects that have no equal. (See also detail on page 122.)

Terminator 2: Judgement Day:
© 1991, Tri-Star Pictures.
Courtesy: Industrial Light &
Magic.

micros to mainframes, are being used to create
animations, and when used correctly, provide a cost-
effective solution to many design applications.

Special effects

The most sophisticated examples of animated
computer graphics are found in special effects
sequences for films. Such techniques are employed
when live action or models are unable to cope with
the fantastic scenarios often included in modern film
scripts. For example, in the 1989 film *The Abyss*, the
script called for a snake-like creature (made from
water) to appear from a large pool of sea water.
Obviously, physical models were out of the question,
but 3D computer graphics and the expertise of
Industrial Light & Magic (ILM), who were responsible
for creating the computer animated sequences,
provided a viable and exciting alternative.

Approximately 70 seconds of computer animation
were integrated into a five-minute live-action
sequence. This involved incredible detailed modelling
for the sea-creature, which at one stage transformed
into an animated human face made from water. But
the effectiveness with which the computer-generated
scenes were composited with the live action, was due
to the environment maps that reflected the creature's
surroundings into its surface. These supplied vital
visual cues that convinced the viewer that the
creature was really in the studio.

Industrial Light & Magic have secured a world
lead in the area of special effects, and their 1991 film,
Terminator 2: Judgement Day, contains the most
sophisticated mixture of computer graphics with live
action produced to date. Many of the scenes call for
seamless transitions of a walking computer-generated
humanoid into a live actor, showing the
complementary changes from synthetic clothes into
real clothes. Even when one knows the computer

148 techniques used in the sequences, the images are so powerful that it is hard to believe they are synthetic.

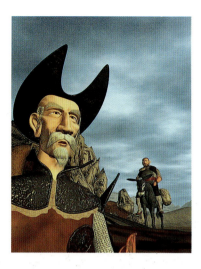

CASE STUDY: *DON QUIXOTE*

In 1990 Videosystem (Paris) made the decision to undertake a major computer animation project based on the windmill episode from Cervantes' universal work *Don Quixote*. Although Videosystem was used to preparing video and computer animation sequences for French television, this project would be the largest they had attempted and was assigned to François Garnier to direct. He decided to turn Don Quixote into the archetypal explorer of the realm of make-believe, in which computer graphics expresses the magic of its ambiguities and multiple transformations.

Working from a detailed storyboard which described almost three minutes of animation, a soundtrack was produced which would help the animators create realistic lip movements. The soundtrack was analysed to identify the frame numbers where important syllables occurred; these frame numbers, together with the sound, could be repeatedly played back to obtain lip synchronization.

Apart from the windmills, which did not present any real modelling problems, the storyboard called

With traditional animation the cartoon characters only exist as line drawings on paper or cel, while in 3D computer animation each character has an independent geometric definition stored within the computer. So, when Videosystem decided to undertake their *Don Quixote* project, an important phase concerned the design and digitization of every feature of the animation, which included the two central human characters, their horses, several windmills, and detailed 3D landscapes.

To achieve this, a variety of modelling techniques were used, including real-time interactive software, and the construction of physical models; in particular the human heads, which were digitized with a 3D digitizer.

TDI-Explore's Artic software and SGI 380 VGX Power Series workstations were used to undertake the animation and rendering.
Courtesy: François Garnier (Director), Videosystem (Paris).

for two humans (Don Quixote and his assistant) a horse and a donkey, all of which had to be modelled in 3D. As the human heads were to be seen in close-up it was decided to physically model them larger than life-size, and use a 3D digitizer to capture their surface geometry. These models were first covered with a mesh of polygons whose size changed as the surface detail became finer.

Using TDI-Explore's Artic software the heads were input, together with other 3D elements from detailed drawings. Then with the aid of Silicon Graphics 380 VGX Power Series workstations, four animators were able to build the individual scenes and review their sequences in real-time. This form of line-testing was evaluated in wireframe which provided the necessary visual cues.

Every feature of the scene required extensive use of texture mapping which gave the animation a rich sense of detail; this was further enhanced by selecting a palette of colours to create a realistic warm level of illumination. The accompanying illustrations confirm the success of this aspect.

The speed of the workstations enabled the animators to evaluate different camera positions and moves in real-time, then short sequences could be rendered and played back to review their effectiveness.

Finally, the individual scenes were rendered and edited, and combined with the soundtrack and specially written music. As the animation was to be shown on film as well as video, it was only a question of repeating the rendering phase at a higher resolution to obtain a 35 mm cine film version.

Don Quixote is a landmark in the history of computer animation, and received an award at Imagina's film festival in Monte Carlo in 1991.

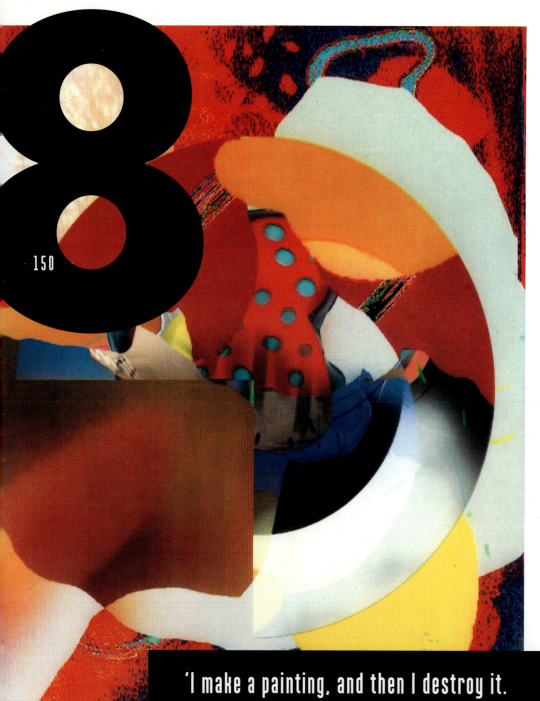

'I make a painting, and then I destroy it.
But nothing is lost. The red destroyed in one place
turns up in another.

PABLO PICASSO

8 Art

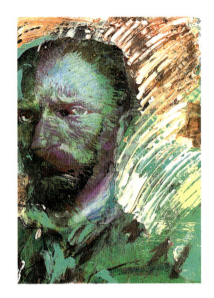

Above: Although American artist Jim Valentine discovered his artistic skills with traditional media, he now explores the hidden talents of a Canon Colour Laser Copier. And as this image shows, Jim is discovering a vital and powerful new medium for artists and illustrators.
Courtesy: Jim Valentine.

Left: A detail from a direct RGB video print-out of work generated in the Harry system by Japanese artist Akira Hasegawa.
Courtesy: Akira Hasegawa/CPM Planning, Komatsu, Japan.

INTRODUCTION

During the past one hundred years the mechanistic world of the industrial revolution has been left behind, and has been replaced by a technology-driven world where radio, television and telephone signals have become the media for global communication; and virtually everywhere the ubiquitous computer is taking a central role.

These developments have had a profound effect on human activity. Where previous generations were concerned with farming, craft, trade and commercial work, today's complex world is about world banking, international stock exchanges, integrated transport networks, food distribution, satellite communications, automated factories and electronic media. Every new generation finds themselves in a world far more complex than that of their predecessors, and each generation rewrites the cultural standards that they believe are relevant to their time.

Such evolution has had a major influence upon all forms of artistic expression. For instance, Igor Stravinsky revealed new expressive dynamic forces in his compositions; Henry Moore's sculptures demonstrated that surface detail was superficial to his bold abstract forms; and Picasso educated us to look at familiar objects from several simultaneous views. The urge to discover new channels for human expression continues to this day, with inventive forces at work in every area of creativity.

There are no written rules that decide what is good or bad; what is genius, and what is mediocre; or what is the result of depression or madness. We can express our emotions, fears, visions, or views of a subject using almost any medium. Our creations may be derided by others, or they may be appreciated and enjoyed.

COMPUTER ART

Within a very short period of time computer graphics has joined this maelstrom of creativity. It has provided the creative mind with feats of artistic agility. Imaginary paint can be applied to a digital canvas with amazing speed. No longer has an image to be formed from single brush strokes: it can be formed from a collage of images; it can be created with textured paint; and it can be created in such a way that every brush stroke is aided and abetted by a computer program.

The world of art is our creation. We have made the rules – in fact, we have arranged that there are no rules. There are no guidelines dictating that an artist must labour for so many hours before a masterpiece can be created. And there are no rules

that guarantee that anyone will appreciate their work. However, the financial system that governs every facet of modern life does have rules. Its internal forces can decide what is 'good', what is 'trivial', what is 'fashionable', and what will 'sell'. However, financial considerations are incidental to this analysis. We are only concerned with how the computer can extend or enhance our need to express internal thoughts, desires and emotions.

We have seen in previous chapters how the computer has revealed totally new ways of developing designs. We have discovered that in some cases, such as type and print, it has revolutionized an entire technology. In other areas, it has complemented existing processes, and wherever it has surfaced, it has introduced new levels of creative freedom. Therefore, we can expect computers to have a similar effect on the world of art.

Another question that needs answering concerns the location of computer art in the established hierarchy of traditional art. For instance, should computer-generated art be compared to Van Gogh, Rembrandt, Renoir or Dali? One response to this is why shouldn't it? Why should the medium of oil on canvas be superior to ink-jet on paper? It is the author's opinion that the medium used by the artist is immaterial: any analysis must be made on the basis of the image, and only the image.

Prior to computer art, the art world embraced many other forms of artistic expression stimulated by our twentieth-century culture. For instance, Pop Art revealed pictures of soup tins, enlargements of comic strips and multi-media collages of actual household objects, and the spectrum of art had to be broadened to encompass these new images. Nowadays, computer artists are inviting us to embrace a new form of imagery that is so revolutionary it is difficult to comprehend all of the ramifications. The medium of digital circuits is still very young and unexplored and is already forcing us to ask some very searching questions about its use.

WHERE IS THE IMAGE?

Visit any art gallery and you will discover a variety of paintings and drawings decorating its walls. The pictures might be on canvas, paper or wood, and produced using oils, watercolour or gouache. They are probably signed and dated to establish their authenticity, and normally there is no confusion about whether the pictures are originals or copies. Basically, we can supply coordinates to fix every image in space and time.

However, introducing computers into the world of art raises some very interesting questions: for example, when a paint system is used to create an image, where does the final image exist? Is it on the display screen, within the computer's memory, or does it only exist when a hard copy is made? To answer these questions it is necessary to return to the conventional physical image and attempt to discover its location.

Paints are nothing more than materials that absorb and reflect light of different wavelengths, and when a painting is illuminated with daylight we

When Jim Valentine saw a Canon Colour Laser Copier for the first time, he did not see a colour copying machine standing before him, but an exciting new medium that incorporated every conceivable illustration technique. The computer-based technology, with its simple 'user-friendly' interface, has been harnessed by Jim to create an original visual language.
Courtesy: Jim Valentine.

Don Miller teaches art at the University of Wisconsin, River Falls in the USA, but his images are known around the world. In recent years he has explored ways of incorporating computer graphics into his image making, for which he uses an Amiga 1000 microcomputer, a high-resolution monitor, and a monochrome video camera.

The video camera and digitizing software enable him to input photographs, which are then manipulated by introducing graphic elements such as lines, colours, shapes and textures. The final images are output using a Xerox 4020 ink-jet printer.

His images consist of an integration of organic forms derived from human, animal, and or landscape elements with geometric elements that have mechanical or machine references. The tension between opposites is central to his form of image making.

Chindi Frieze #1 (below) was designed on an Amiga 1000 and output to a Xerox ink-jet printer.
Courtesy: Don Miller.

experience a sensation of colour patterns known as 'the image'. This coloured image, however, is the result of a complex chain of events starting with different light-reflecting materials, a source of illumination, and an observer who declares the existence of the image. The final event of seeing takes place somewhere within our brains and becomes integrated with other sensory data sets and memories. If we move the original canvas we must follow it if we wish to continue seeing the image. Furthermore, if we move the canvas away from a source of daylight and illuminate it with tungsten lamps or fluorescent tubes the colour balance of the picture is altered.

In the case of an image created on a paint system the mechanism is completely different. Although we 'see' an image on the display screen, this is actually the result of an illusion, because the screen is being continuously refreshed to keep the coloured phosphors glowing. The original source of the image is no longer something physical we can touch, smell and weigh like a canvas. Whenever we wish to see a computer image, an electrical process must be activated which results in an image. Disconnect the computer from its source of energy and the image disappears. Furthermore, connect several display screens to the same computer and a number of identical original images are seen.

The display process involves hardware in the form of electrical circuits and complementary data which might be electrical or magnetic in nature. The data probably encodes colour levels for each pixel, and the circuits translate the codes into some useful physical output. Both data and circuitry are vital in the chain of events for creating an image. Therefore, the source of the image is a process rather than a physical thing. A computer no longer needs us to maintain the source of an image as a physical

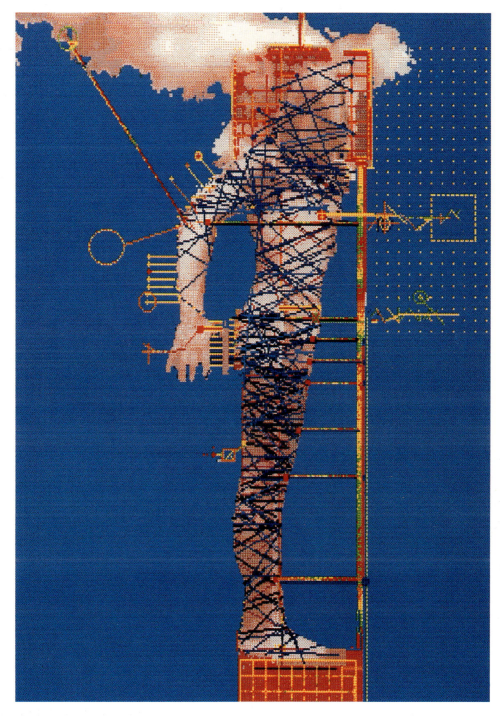

Don Miller's *Sentinel #1* was
created on an Amiga 1000
using DIGI-VIEW and DELUXE
PAINT, and output to a Xerox
C150 ink-jet printer.
Courtesy: Don Miller.

artefact, as it can be stored as a set of rules.

This implies that uniqueness may no longer be relevant to synthetic images as it is an easy exercise to copy a computer process: in many cases it is nothing more than copying one magnetic disk onto another. Therefore, if an artist creates an image on one computer, any number of perfect copies can be made and replicated upon other computers. Obviously, if the artist wishes to guarantee that the source of the image remains unique, then he or she must ensure that no one gains access to the machine's circuits, otherwise the process can be stolen, and not even a computer will be able to distinguish between the two.

As the source of the image is a process rather than an object, the process can be employed to create different interpretations of the image. For example, the image can be displayed upon a screen; it can also be output onto film stock, video tape, paper or even canvas. Perhaps this will be the only way of ensuring that the image is guaranteed a place alongside other works of art, because if the technology that is used to interpret the process becomes redundant, the source of the image could also die.

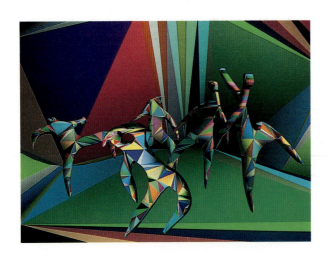

Charles Csuri's involvement with computer graphics began in 1967 when he drew images on a cathode ray tube using an interactive light pen. His enthusiasm for this new medium engaged him in many projects including an interactive animation environment, computer sculpture, and interpolation procedures. This early work took the form of line drawings, but with the introduction of raster graphics he explored the extra dimension of colour, and virtual 3D worlds.
Courtesy: Charles Csuri.

156

THE 3D EYE

Traditionally, artists are used to the disciplines of preparing intermediate sketches before fixing parameters such as the horizon line, vanishing points, centres of interest, illumination and shadows. And on completion of the image there is no opportunity to interactively change any of the features, apart from applying fresh paint.

Photographers, on the other hand, exploit the fact that they can capture on film any number of views of a scene before returning to their darkroom to isolate a portion of the most promising negative. But apart from this form of post-processing, their camera can be placed and oriented in space with relative ease. The scene can be enhanced with extra illumination, and some features can be carefully positioned to capture the desired drama. Nevertheless, they are always hindered by reflections and shadows caused by their own interaction with the scene. They might not always be able to position their camera in an optimum position, and they certainly have little control over natural phenomena such as sunlight, clouds, shadows and the weather.

Artists who have explored the virtual 3D world within computers have discovered a universe over which they have complete artistic control. They can hand-craft the objects in the scene which can be assigned real and imaginary surface properties; they have control over illumination levels, positions and colours of lights. Objects can be placed anywhere in space, as it is a world free from gravity. But one of the major features the virtual approach offers is that when the picture has been taken, the artist still has complete control over the process of creating the image. Objects can be moved, light sources changed and the camera can even be repositioned to obtain an optimum view.

But unlike a real camera, the virtual camera can be placed anywhere in space and is able to view the scene from physically impossible positions. The fact that the image is the result of a process means that any internal features can be fine-tuned to capture one or many views of the 3D configuration. A natural development of this form of image creation is animated 3D art, where various artists have already explored imaginary worlds. Such work is often achieved using standard software, but many artists are willing to master the skills of programming to develop their own style of image making.

'I am interested in the idea of infinite space and depth and I am intrigued by the immense expanse of space which is beyond time. There is also an inner and external space and the combinations of a micro and macro universe. I try to express a conceptual and mythological space that may represent deep, inner problems and mysteries.

I struggle very hard to understand how I can symbolically and metaphorically deal with issues and questions that humans have been concerned about since the beginning of time such as life, death, mortality, love, power, courage, time, consciousness itself, spirituality, comedy and so it goes.' (Charles Csuri, Imagina 1991)
Courtesy: Charles Csuri.

3D MODELLING

Any computer system involves a mixture of hardware and software. The hardware includes the computer with its memory and central processing unit, and any associated input/output peripherals such as digitizers, video cameras, scanners, graph plotters, video recorders and imagesetters. The software covers the operating system, user interfaces, application programs and programming languages.

Each design discipline employs various techniques for representing their graphic structures within the computer's world. In the case of paint systems, images are held as a matrix of pixel elements describing primary colour components. In typography, bitmaps and Bézier curves are used to represent letterforms. Architectural models may use files of annotated line drawings for 2D schematics, and 3D geometric descriptions of buildings constructed from polygons. Animators employ video images, line drawings, photographic textures, Bézier surface patches and programs for making special effects.

The problem for any artists wanting to create 3D scenes within a computer concerns the techniques that can be used to translate their own ideas into a form acceptable to the computer. To a certain extent this is always limited by the various physical features of computers. For instance, the size of a computer's memory and disk units will always impose an upper limit to any 3D environment constructed in a computer. Similarly, the computer's speed dictates whether an image is created in 0.02 seconds or two days. But apart from these restrictions the most important issue for the artist is how to represent complex physical phenomena and abstract concepts.

Very early computer artists had to work with small-memory computers that were slow and had to be programmed using scientific languages. The only output medium was via a graph plotter, and in general, their images were constructed from lines. As computer technology advanced, artists found that they could explore more complex visual structures, and nowadays technology is no longer the primary problem. However, artists still have to rely on a limited repertoire of modelling tools to build their 3D environments, and although these are very advanced, no one would ever claim that they are complete.

The simplest modelling scheme is to construct objects from collections of polygons, which basically develop a surface skin defining the object's boundary. The inside of the object is empty and theoretically the skin has no thickness. Architects use this boundary technique for building their models, and take the trouble to construct interior walls, floors, ceilings, stairways, windows and doors. These surfaces can be coloured, textured and illuminated, and create very realistic images.

The artist can also employ the same modelling scheme to construct elements in their 3D world, but the polygonal surfaces do have their limitations. For example, an artist may wish to build a panoramic landscape from thousands of glass spheres of different colours. Spheres are not made from flat polygons; a sphere's surface is smooth, continuous, and has a fixed radius of curvature.

Fortunately for the artist, there are many other

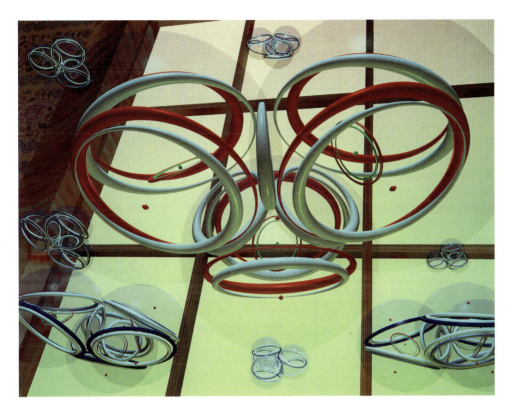

Kenneth Snelson's art has been seen throughout the world in publications, group shows and one-person shows for 25 years. He has been recognized internationally for his work and received many awards. His art is focused on questions of structure and the varied ways separate parts can join together to make a whole. His best-known outdoor sculptures are constructed of rigid steel bars connected with wire rope.

In the late 1980s he experimented with the emerging technology of raster graphics and invested in a Silicon Graphics workstation and Wavefront graphics software.

Invasion (above) is a fantasy image in which molecules of cyclopropane, an anaesthetic gas, float in an otherwise normal domestic scene. This image has been scanned from the original transparency which was rendered to a resolution of 8,000 lines.
Courtesy: Kenneth Snelson.

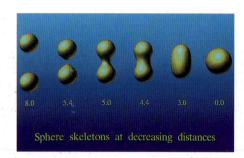

Sphere skeletons at decreasing distances

Brian and Geoff Wyvill have pioneered the use of soft objects in computer animation, where objects are constructed from collections of soft spheres and ellipsoids. In this illustration it is possible to see how intermediate forms are created as the distance between two spheres is decreased.
Courtesy: Brian and Geoff Wyvill.

users who require smooth surfaces, and special techniques have been developed to support modelling schemes using surface patches such as Bézier and B-spline patches. The car industry, in particular, employs such techniques and the artist can also access these modelling tools.

However, objects built from polygons or patches only form a skin – they are no use for applications where the object's interior has to be exposed. To model surfaces and interior volumes, another technique is used called Constructive Solid Geometry (CSG). This employs the mathematical equations for a planar surface, sphere, cylinder, cone and helix which, when combined, are capable of producing extremely complex structures. The artist William Latham used this technique to build objects in *The Conquest of Form, Evolution of Form* and *Mutations*.

Because CSG objects are represented by equations, programs can exploit a variety of geometric and spatial features that are difficult using other strategies. For example, it is easy to distinguish between the outside and inside of a CSG object, which means that they can be coloured and textured separately. Portions of the objects can be cut away, or objects can be pushed through one another.

Another technique that permits the modelling of smooth continuous surfaces employs 'meta balls' or 'isopotential surfaces': these are useful for building structures and surfaces possessing an elastic skin. As an illustration, consider a scenario in which two spheres approach one another. While they remain a certain distance apart they retain their spherical characteristics. But when they pass a certain limit they begin to influence one another by distorting their surface topology. Eventually, they fuse together to form some inbetween volume that depends on the distance between the two spheres. This form of modelling has been used by Yoichiro Kawaguchi in his animated sequences using meta balls, and by Brian Wyvill using soft objects.

But how are trees, grass, water, smoke, clouds, mountains, fur, flowers and fire modelled? In computer graphics these are classified as natural phenomena and unfortunately, no one modelling scheme can build them all. A plethora of techniques has evolved over the last decade that attempts to solve some of these problems. For example, fractals can be used to generate 3D mountain terrains and 2D textures for clouds and fire. A fractal is a mathematical concept but it does appear in an approximate form in certain natural forms. For instance, a tree without leaves is easily recognized even at a distance. But imagine breaking off one of its major branches and planting it in the ground; it too would look similar to the original tree when viewed at a suitable distance. This same process could be repeated two or three times to smaller branches before it would become obvious that we were looking at a single twig. Because of this effect, the tree is said to possess 'self-similarity'.

With the aid of some simple computer programs it is possible to build fractal-like objects such as mountains by first describing its gross characteristics, which may be nothing more than a triangle placed on the ground. This triangle can then be divided into

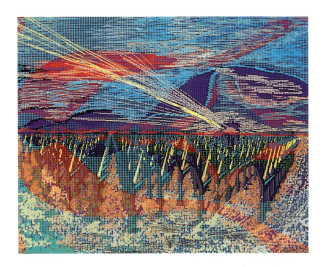

Mike King's creative skills are evident in this and the image on page 162, where 2D painted scenes are contrasted with 3D sculptures. His enthusiasm for computer graphics is reflected in the software tools he has designed at the City Polytechnic in London where he teaches computer graphics to Diploma students. His pioneering 'Sculptor' software system was used by the artist William Latham, and has continued to evolve in a demanding academic environment.
Courtesy: Mike King, The City Polytechnic.

Courtesy: Mike King, The City
Polytechnic.

four similar smaller triangles whose corners are pulled up and down randomly by the computer to create a crumpled effect. By dividing these triangles into similar smaller triangles, and continuing the process for a few levels, it is possible to create very realistic mountains. From a single triangle and a few rules one can build entire mountain ranges. Particle systems have been used to model trees, fur and fire. Atmospheric effects such as haze, fog and smoke are modelled as procedures, which brings us back to the idea of a process used to describe an image.

Modelling is not a coherent methodology where anything can be created; it is a mixture of techniques that have been developed over recent years to solve problems as they have arisen. It is still an area of investigation that is far from complete, and one over which artists and designers will be able to exert considerable influence.

ANIMATED ART

The computer provides the perfect environment for creating animated works of art: not in the sense of cartoons – although there is no reason why this should not be so – but perhaps in the use of animated colour palettes, metamorphosis effects, cyclic events, or even elaborate choreographed sequences. Traditional media have limited the artist to one static image, but with real-time computer graphics this is no longer the case. Time has become another colour on the artist's palette.

This means that the artist must develop a close relationship with computer technology, especially if they wish to explore territory not yet supported by existing software. Someone must design and develop the process in the form of computer programs, and as historical events have shown, the fine artist is suited to undertake these tasks.

INTERACTIVE ART

If a synthetic image is nothing more than a process being executed, what happens if this process is disturbed by the observer? As the computer is capable of changing any parameter within its memory whether it be a colour intensity, a geometric dimension, or the location of an imaginary camera, it is only a question of computer performance and the interactive interface to make the images interactive.

For example, given some simple video equipment it would be possible to detect and locate people approaching a screen containing a refreshed synthetic image. This data could be input to the program responsible for the image and used to modify various image-sensitive features. Colours could be altered in the vicinity of the observer, or a train of events executed that temporarily disturbs the equilibrium of the image. The artist is thus able to modify any feature of the image database.

VIRTUAL ART WORLDS

The technology of Virtual Reality will have a profound effect on computer art as it will allow the artist to construct imaginary worlds where transparent 3D space will become the medium of the artist. No longer will paint have to be applied to surfaces – the

The work of Twin Planet
Communications in Tokyo is a
combination of live footage,
2D graphics and the use of the
Paintbox to edit frame by
frame. The RGB video print-out
below is by Akira Hasegawa,
who coined the phrase 'Digital
Play' to categorize his work.
*Courtesy: Akira Hasegawa/CPM
Planning, Komatsu, Japan.*

artist will be able to paint directly onto empty space. Obviously, no real paint will be used in this process, but within the computer's circuits, codes will be stored and rules written that will simulate this imaginary world.

New software environments will need to be developed to allow the artist to manipulate space, colour, texture, surfaces and volumes in a way never before considered. Such environments will provide an experimental studio where these worlds can be designed over a period of time without any physical resource apart from an empty room. Paintings and sculptures can be started and then put to one side and continued at a later date. The computer's circuits provide a perfect environment where these worlds can be stored and explored by the artist at any time.

Several artists will be able to share these virtual worlds, even though they may be separated physically in space. This would promote projects where different artists could collaborate at a distance and at different times. This space could also be made available to others who might wish to explore it at their leisure. Eventually, one can anticipate the existence of an entire gallery of virtual art created by artists all over the world.

This is an exciting period for the artist, for the computer's involvement is raising important aesthetic issues for the first time: while some members of the art community are trying to decide where the image resides, others are arguing whether computer art is really 'art' at all. But perhaps the most contented artists are those who are using computers to provide society with images that reflect the technological culture of the twentieth century, and an art form that is still in its infancy.

CASE STUDY: 3D COMPUTER SCULPTURE

Traditional sculptors go about their work using techniques such as clay modelling, stone carving, construction and welding. And with the aid of chisels, hammers, welding equipment, saws and grinding tools they purposefully create their sculptures. However, in the world of computer graphics the software modelling tools for constructing 3D objects have been developed to meet the needs of architects and engineers, and any sculptor wanting to use other techniques must either write new programs or find a programmer who will undertake this task.

This is where the medium of computer graphics differs from other media: it creates opportunities for group participation. One such collaboration has involved William Latham and Stephen Todd. Together

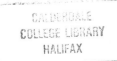

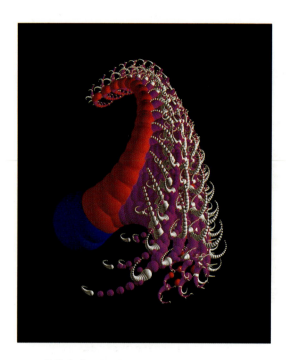

Self-similar structures are easily modelled using ESME, and in this illustration of a fractal horn, (entitled *Recursive Horn*) by William Latham, it is possible to see how a central component has been repeatedly transformed to build a second structure. *Courtesy: William Latham, Stephen Todd and IBM UK Scientific Centre.*

they have evolved a computer environment for modelling and animating a unique style of 3D forms. The original concept started with Latham's early work using Mike King's 'Sculptor' program where he was able to build structures from a choice of graphic primitives such as a tetrahedron, icosahedron, sphere, cone and cylinder, using operations like: beak, scoop, bulge, stretch, slice, add and subtract.

When Latham moved to the IBM UK Scientific Centre as Visiting Computer Artist, he was able to continue his work using IBM's WINSOM (Winchester Solid Modeller) system; this is a powerful rendering package based on Constructive Solid Geometry (CSG), used mainly for data visualization, and has extensive texturing features. Stephen Todd, who is a mathematician at IBM, developed the texturing algorithms for WINSOM, and ESME which provides an interactive programming environment.

As with other applications of computer graphics, the role of the computer is to set the colour of every pixel forming the image. In most 2D applications the artist interactively sets these colours using paint programs, but with 3D applications, where the objects forming the scene can move, a process based on a set of rules is required. This process introduces a virtual software paradigm to support a world in which forms can be constructed and manipulated, and eventually rendered onto some display device. But this software only becomes really useful when one is able to modify parameters that influence the outcome of the process; moreover, the software becomes incredibly powerful when these modifications are automatically undertaken by itself.

WINSOM provides the virtual world in which 3D structures are defined. These are built by combining together primitives such as sphere, helix, cone, cylinder and torus, using the logical operators add, subtract and difference. As any primitive can be scaled, translated and rotated it is possible to build highly organic structures. For example, a twisted horn-like form can be created by first using a helix whose radius reduces as it spirals vertically. If this helix is used as a control curve, then a collection of spheres can be positioned along this curve whose radii reduce in step with that of the helix. If the spheres touch one another this would appear as a string of beads of reducing size, but CSG allows primitives to intersect, which means that thousands of spheres can be arranged so that they successively overlap to create an apparently smooth surface.

ESME is like any other computer language in that it has a formal syntax, but differs in that it possesses commands to directly manipulate CSG operations. For example, the instruction CUBE(1) provides the user with a unit cube located at the origin of the world space. And there are similar commands for cylinder, sphere, torus etc. When an ESME function is executed, the user must input the class of CSG structure to manipulate; the number of times this structure is to be repeated; and the type of geometric transform to be applied to each repeat. ESME also allows the parameters to change in time, which is how an animation sequence is obtained. The animator then choreographs a scene by adjusting the parameter settings to change as the timescale is

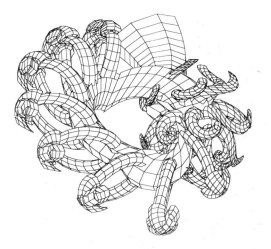

This ESME function is capable of building a horn-like structure depending upon the values of the three parameters input by the user.
Courtesy: William Latham, Stephen Todd and IBM UK Scientific Centre.

The 'Mutator' software presents the user with nine mutations from an original specification from which one can be selected for further mutations. The user proceeds along an evolutionary path until a desired form has been selected.
Courtesy: William Latham, Stephen Todd and IBM UK Scientific Centre.

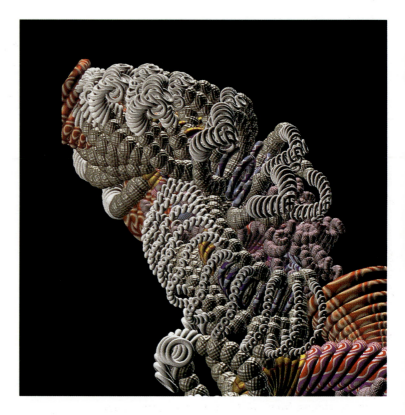

This computer sculpture by William Latham is the result of several cycles of mutation using the 'Mutator' system.
Courtesy: William Latham, Stephen Todd and IBM UK Scientific Centre.

stepped along in frame increments.

WINCAT (Winchester Colour And Texture) is the software module for applying colour and textures to the CSG structures. These include diffuse and specular surfaces, and transparent and luminous objects. The texturing features include bump mapping, image mapping and solid textures.

William Latham prepares his animation scripts by calling upon previously written functions and incorporating new functions, which are evaluated by playing back low-resolution line tests. When these are satisfactory, the final high-resolution anti-aliased sequence is rendered.

Latham's recent work has investigated the processes of evolution and mutation as a method for creating computer sculptures, and is called 'Mutator'. The designer begins by constructing a parameterized object where each parameter will have a range of values to choose from. 'Mutator' then displays nine versions of this object that are derived from the initial choice of parameters. One of these is selected, and the other eight rejected. The 'lucky' one is also allowed to seed nine new mutations, from which another is selected until a satisfactory sculpture is obtained. Facilities even exist where two forms are 'married' to create children who inherit their parents' characteristics.

This type of collaboration has been very fruitful for Latham and Todd, and has resulted in some of the most extraordinary static and animated sculptures to be created with the aid of computers. Hopefully this will continue and also inspire others to initiate research projects where artists, sculptors and designers can work creatively with mathematicians and computer programmers.

'You can never plan the future by the past.'

EDMUND BURKE

9 The Future

PREDICTING THE FUTURE

Fortunately the future cannot be predicted: however, tomorrow's world is not completely determined by chaotic events. The human inertia to change ensures some level of continuity, and therefore up to a point, permits projecting what is happening in today's world into future years.

It is obvious, however, that computers are here to stay. Moreover, they have made such a positive impression in design applications, it would be unthinkable to continue without their assistance. So perhaps what really needs addressing in this chapter is how computers will continue to evolve and what extra benefits they will bring.

We must also be careful that we do not become blinkered by computer technology, for it will not just be developments in processors that will dictate the future of computer graphics, but parallel developments in software, new methods of interacting with computer systems, new peripherals for the input and output of images, and the important issues of standards and the control of colour. Neither can we ignore the intersection of computer technology with other technologies. However, let us address these areas one at a time and attempt to understand what impact future developments will bring to computer graphics.

COMPUTER PROCESSORS

During previous years there has been a continuous increase in computer speed, which is bound to spiral upwards. But one of the restrictions of VLSI processors (see Glossary) is that their speed is governed by an internal clock controlling the execution rate of instructions. This is being steadily increased, but a more effective method of improving instruction throughput is to build computer systems from multiple processors. Nowadays, such machines are commonplace, containing two to several thousand individual processors, which offer awesome levels of raw speed. Perhaps one day the idea of MIPS or GIPS (Giga Instructions Per Second) will be obsolete and another unit relating it to the neuron capacity of the human brain will be devised.

The reason why such levels of computer performance are necessary for computer graphics should now be obvious. When a full-colour image is held within a computer it is represented by billions of bits of data which all need manipulating, preferably at high speed. It is this desire to see images move without jumping or hesitating that demands high processing speeds. In 3D applications it can be frustrating to wait several minutes while the computer renders a new view of the model. Therefore, as other complex applications emerge, the demand for even

Page 170: Simulating natural phenomena presents an exciting challenge to researchers in computer graphics: on the one hand, a mechanism must be found to model the phenomenon, and on the other, a technique must be able to animate it. This image of 3D clouds was produced by Bhash Naidoo, an MSc student at the University of Teeside.
Courtesy: Bhash Naidoo.

172

higher levels of processing performance will surface. As computers become faster, it seems natural that memory capacities will expand to meet the demand for larger and more sophisticated software packages.

The above argument assumes that images will continue to be stored as pixels. There may be alternative processes, but for the moment the pixel approach is the most successful and will probably remain for some time to come. However, we must expect new revolutionary technologies that could one day replace everything that is used today. Hopefully, that day is some time away, as a reasonable level of stability is needed for the long-term success of any developing technology.

PERIPHERALS

Great technological strides have been made during the last five years in resolving the problem of scanning colour images into a computer and the output of full-colour pictures onto paper or film. The quality of this hardware is extraordinary and employs very sophisticated electronics and incredible mixtures of chemistry, science, mechanics and optics. The technology of colour laser copiers is rapidly improving, and laser imagesetters, laser scanners, and ink-jet plotters have all surprised users of computer graphics systems by their high quality.

Colour scanners and colour printers are relatively new devices. Some are very expensive and large pieces of equipment, and it would be comforting to believe that such hardware will develop into smaller and cheaper units, and become standard peripherals for everyone in the near future. Scanning in very high-resolution images is also a time-consuming process, especially when a project requires the input of several images. Many minutes are needed to mechanically track a light sensor across an image to retreive the primary colour separations. It does not seem beyond the realm of possibility that this process is reduced to a matter of seconds using a non-mechanical approach. However, for the moment these delays must be tolerated.

Another feature of computer graphics systems to which we have all adjusted is the need to work with a large desk-mounted monitor. Many designers using a paint system for the first time need some time to adjust to the way electronic images are painted. No longer can they look at their hand holding some drawing implement, but must now gaze at the computer display screen, which contains the electronic marks resulting from the way they move a stylus over the surface of a digitizing tablet.

However, we must anticipate changes to this mode of working. Flat panel displays using liquid crystals are already used in car instrumentation, calculators and lap-top computers. Even full-colour television sets have been built from similar flat panel hardware, therefore it is highly likely that one day designers will be able to draw directly onto a horizontal display surface very much like a conventional drawing board. This would transform the way we interact with graphics packages and make computer systems very similar to traditional drawing processes.

NEW USER INTERFACES

The keyboard still plays an important role in communicating with computers and probably will continue to do so for some time to come, even though the mouse has greatly diminished its use in many interactive graphics applications. Eventually, however, voice communication should provide a very powerful mode of interacting with machines. Synthetic speech and voice recognition technology already exists, and perhaps it will only be a short period of time before this becomes sufficiently sophisticated to allow users to talk to their systems without using keyboards. Naturally, this will demand highly sophisticated systems and interfaces to cope with all of the associated problems introduced by syntax, semantics, and accents, yet in spite of these problems, this rapidly developing technology opens the way to some exciting scenarios.

ACCURATE COLOUR CONTROL

The accurate control of colour is vital to any designer whether they are using computers or not. Even in photography, the control of colour is not a trivial issue: colour bias in film stock varies from one manufacturer to another; the colour balance of photographs is very sensitive to the mode of illumination; and the final developing process requires careful monitoring to ensure chemical processes remain consistent.

Colour printing processes share similar problems, making it very difficult to guarantee perfect colour reproduction. In many circumstances it is not vital that high levels of colour consistency are maintained. For example, newspapers containing a few colour photographs cannot afford to employ sophisticated printing processes. The paper quality does not make it easy to reproduce high quality images, neither does

the speed with which the paper is printed; and the life of the average newspaper is measured in hours, and does not warrant such attention to detail.

On the other hand, colour control is central to the fashion industry. And in advertising, the colour of a cup of tea, a glass of beer, or a company logo are vital design issues. Also, now that computer graphics with its associated digital technology has become part of the design process, system designers have rapidly become aware of the problems that have always existed within the industry.

But the introduction of computers into the design world may, at last, help resolve many of these problems. The central role of the computer integrates a number of different technologies. For example, images are input via different types of scanners, from video cameras to laser photocopiers. These images are then displayed upon colour monitors. Intermediate images may be output upon ink-jet printers or colour copiers. Final colour images may be output to colour negative film or split into four-colour separations using laser imagesetters. With all of this technology it is easy to understand why colours change from the input to output stages.

However, the computer provides a perfect opportunity for resolving these issues. What is needed is a colour space which will be accepted as a standard throughout the industry and will be the internal format for all software operations. Every input device to a computer graphics system will then have its own translation tables for converting its signals into this internal format, and vice versa for the output devices. This move towards device-independent colour specifications is already underway, and it may not be too long before we see some positive approaches to resolving the accurate control of colour.

EDUCATION

In the 1980s very few art and design colleges possessed computer technology for teaching computer graphics. However, with the arrival of low-cost PC systems and affordable software the scene suddenly changed, and undergraduates were exposed to some of the computer graphics techniques being used commercially. Nowadays, there is no real reason why students should not receive some exposure to DTP systems and paint programs before leaving college. Some students even have the opportunity of becoming *au fait* with up-to-date professional equipment during their studies.

There are an increasing number of institutes that offer excellent postgraduate courses where specialist topics in computer graphics can be pursued to some depth. These courses have required substantial funding to acquire skilled staff and suitable hardware and software. In many cases industry has either donated or heavily discounted their products to assist colleges in taking this first step.

Unfortunately, digital technology is evolving so rapidly it is impossible for the academic world to keep abreast of every development. But art and design departments are not alone in this respect: virtually every branch of learning – be it astronomy, music, physics or medicine – has been influenced one way or another by computers. This is the price that must be paid for the benefits computers bring. They cannot simply be a feature of industrial and commercial practices: our educational system has no choice but to adapt to industry's expectations and provide computer-literate students.

This is easier said than done, for computers are not like calculators; they are not just used when they are convenient to perform some arithmetic problem. Computers have provided an electronic medium that has integrated channels of information that hitherto were unique and separate. Today, multi-media systems are being developed that process images, sound, voice and text. Computers can communicate with other computers via modems; they can be interfaced to telephone and fax lines; they process images in real-time, and advances in neural networks are rapidly taking us towards 'intelligent' machines.

Increasingly, digital technology will continue to impact upon the way designers apply their creative visual skills, for as this digital medium evolves it will offer new and unique solutions to design problems. Obviously, the traditional skills of typeface design, graphic design, colour, technical illustration, perspective drawing and so on will continue, but they will have to accommodate new working processes

4. Art GmbH, MUNICH

It is inevitable that computer graphics will influence technical illustration techniques. As this synthetic image shows, a modern renderer can produce highly detailed images using the effect of semi-transparent surfaces.
Courtesy: Created by Vierte Art in Munich using Wavefront Visualizer software.

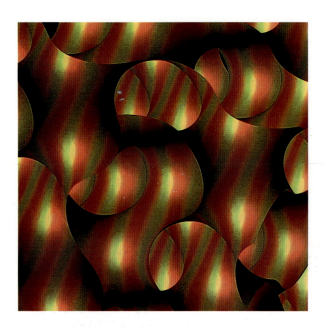

This unusual image illustrates how mathematical concepts can be treated graphically, using IBM Data Explorer. In this example we see a periodic minimal surface which forms labyrinths of curves and holes resembling Emmental cheese.
Data: Prof Ian McKay, Birkbeck College.
Visualization: Jacub Wejchert, IBM European Visualization Centre, Winchester.

and explore new application areas.

Design skills must be brought to bear upon new technologies that employ graphics. Moreover, designers must become involved in human-computer interface issues where screen layout, colour, menus, typefaces, and interaction are vital to the effectiveness of a computer system. They must understand and know how to exploit the graphic features offered by computers, such as real-time interaction, animation, 3D graphics and video. But to achieve this they must complement their understanding of traditional media with this technological medium.

Such revolutionary developments are difficult for both industry and education: for neither can adjust instantly to these changes, and it will take some time before either side can claim to have totally embraced computers. But during this time of transition, one can expect major changes to occur in the way artists, designers, engineers, doctors, lawyers and scientists are trained for their future careers.

SCIENTIFIC VISUALIZATION
Scientists, engineers and mathematicians frequently turn to graphic designers, and in particular technical illustrators, to provide a graphical interpretation of

sets of data, abstract concepts, or cut-away views of three-dimensional objects. Data which is represented graphically is a powerful tool for extracting information, and it seems natural to engage computer graphics in these tasks.

Paint systems provide a simple and direct method for creating a single image or sequence of images for visualizing interiors, assemblies, cut-away views, or graphical interpretations of statistical data, and are frequently used for television graphics.

More complex renderings of 3D objects can be obtained automatically from different views if one is prepared to input the geometry. Sometimes this geometry has already been captured during the original design of an object, and this data can be processed to provide cut-away views, exploded sub-assemblies, or images where different levels of transparency are used to reveal the internal structure. Software employed for computer animation is often used in these applications.

The area of scientific visualization is rapidly providing a wealth of techniques for translating large and complex sets of data into informative images. Such data are often created by computer programs performing a simulation exercise, where equations and algorithms describing some physical system can be evaluated within the confines of the computer's

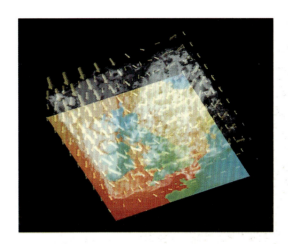

In this image for weather modelling, 2D data are used for water and land surface temperature, which has been colour coded, and 3D data for cloud cover and wind vectors. The software used was IBM Data Explorer.
Data: Dr Sue Ballard, UK Meteorological Office, Bracknell.
Visualization: Jon Tyrrel, IBM UK Scientific Centre, Winchester.

Recovery of oil involves injecting fluid into the reservoir to displace the oil towards the production wells. This image shows water saturation (cyan), gas concentration (yellow) and shale barriers. The software used was IBM Data Explorer. *Data: Dr Jon Barley, BP Research International, Sunbury. Visualization: Dave Williams, IBM European Visualization Centre, Winchester.*

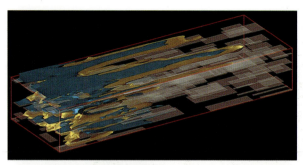

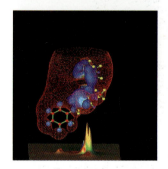

This visualization (using IBM Data Explorer) shows a drug molecule, enalapryl, shown as a ball-and-stick model with two isosurfaces from the calculated electrostatic field, and a rubber sheet depicting the gradient of the field at a given level. *Data: Prof Graham Richards, Oxford University. Visualization: Dr David Collins, IBM European Visualization Centre, Winchester.*

memory. Typical applications include the study of weather phenomena, petroleum geophysics, applied mathematics, astrophysics, aerodynamics and computational chemistry. And one of the major benefits the computer brings to this type of visualization is the ability to depict a scene in three dimensions with animation.

Considerable processing power is required to perform these animations in real-time, but as computer performance is increasing at incredible rates, in the very near future, real-time graphics will be playing a very important role in the computer-human interface.

VIRTUAL REALITY

During these chapters the word 'virtual' has surfaced often; this is because any computer process involves simulating a system by substituting a real thing, such as an image, by an equivalent that has no familiar reality. Obviously, the substitute has an existence, but the simulation process has reduced it to the level of a bubbling universe of digital electrical pulses, where everything is virtual.

The emerging discipline of virtual reality is addressing the issues of real-time human-computer interaction, and provides alternative methods for controlling the computer's simulated world. Instead of using a mouse to control the screen's 2D cursor, an interactive glove can be used to identify positions within the internal virtual 3D space. This involves tracking the position of the user's glove in the real world, and monitoring hand gestures characterized by finger flexions. When these data are used to control the position of a virtual hand in the displayed image, the user can identify features of the 3D model. For example, a 3D computer model could be constructed using this form of interaction through the use of various hand movements.

Developing the concept further involves convincing the user that they are actually inside this imaginary 3D space. This is effected by replacing the user's view of the outside world with a stereoscopic view of the virtual world, which is achieved with a head-mounted display system. This is also tracked by various transducers which inform the computer of the position of the user's head and its orientation. The computer can now supply the user with real-time images that they would see from a particular point in space. When the user's head moves, the images change accordingly, creating the impression that they are physically immersed in this imaginary world.

A computer user fitted with an interactive glove and a head-mounted display can, with suitable

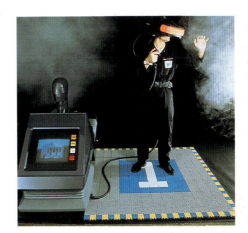

The Virtuality ™ 1000 SU is designed for a user standing or moving within a scanned area, with the Visette ™ visor providing an interface with the virtual world. Interaction with the virtual world is provided by a hand-held unit.
Courtesy: W Industries Ltd, Leicester, England.

The Virtuality ™ Data Glove offers interaction such that the glove may grasp and place models in a virtual world. *Courtesy: W Industries Ltd, Leicester, England.*

software, perform a variety of 3D operations. For instance, it will be possible to model 3D objects and manipulate them interactively by physically adjusting their geometric features. In architectural applications this will allow an architect to explore an imaginary building to assess the effects of repositioning windows, walls and doors. He or she could 'fly' outside the building to obtain realistic 3D views of the structure from anywhere in space.

In another application like fashion, one can imagine the possibility of dressing a virtual mannequin which would apparently be standing in the middle of a room. The fashion designer, suitably equipped with gloves and stereo viewer, could then walk around the mannequin making adjustments to the clothes. Different colour combinations and materials could be compared just as though a real person were standing in the room trying on the different clothes for the designer.

This may sound improbable, but in fact it is rapidly becoming reality. The important aspect of virtual reality systems is not whether it is possible or not, but whether it is useful and cost-effective. We already have the technology to make all of this happen, but it would be too expensive to reap any commercial benefits. Nevertheless, virtual reality is destined to become an important mode of interaction with computer systems. A little more time is required to design new head-mounted display systems and develop the integrated environments within which the user will communicate with the computer.

INTELLIGENT SYSTEMS

The majority of computer systems used by industry today are ordinary processors programmed with conventional programs that ensure that a task is performed accurately and efficiently. For example, all the software associated with the computer graphics tasks described in earlier chapters exploit relatively straightforward sets of rules to achieve their goals. But the arrival of 'intelligent' computer systems will impact upon all types of application areas, including art and design.

Now one must be extremely careful in the use of the word 'intelligent' as we all seem to nurture a personal definition of its meaning, and some people are disturbed by the idea of 'thinking' machines. The reasons for this are understandable as such propositions may undermine religious explanations for human existence, or even conflict with philosophical beliefs that have taken a lifetime of personal development.

My dictionary's entry for 'intelligence' reads: 'the capacity for understanding; ability to perceive and comprehend meaning', which seems acceptable, but what do we really mean by 'understanding' and 'comprehend meaning'? The same dictionary defines 'understanding' as: 'the ability to learn, judge, make decisions, etc'; the entry for 'comprehend' is: 'to understand'; and 'meaning' is defined as: 'the sense or significance of a word, sentence or symbol, etc'.

So using the formal definitions of a dictionary, intelligence is about learning, making decisions, being able to judge, and responding to a vocabulary

These pictures are 2D representations of 3D worlds as experienced in Virtual Reality. The large ball and chess pieces can be interactively manipulated while the operator is manoeuvring in a real-time immersive environment.

Both images feature radiosity, generation of life-like shadowing, surface reflections, and absorption. The images were generated on the 'Provision' system created by Division Ltd.
Courtesy: Clive Jones, Division Ltd, Bristol, UK.

of structured words and symbols, which seems quite reasonable, and activities that could be performed by a computer. At this point, however, other arguments surface, and questions such as: 'But does the computer really know what it's doing, and could it ever experience any emotion?' are asked. To answer such questions one must understand the expressions 'really know' and 'emotion', and this leads us into a recursive maze of semantics.

A major disadvantage for any computer is that they do not look like human beings, and therefore they are easily discriminated against. But every day we talk on the phone to people we have never met; we accept that because they can hold a conversation they are intelligent. So to overcome the problem of physical appearances, perhaps the computer should be heard and not seen, and then we can decide through conversation whether it possesses any degree of intelligence. This test was first proposed by Alan Turing, a brilliant mathematician and computer scientist who anticipated intelligent machines long before the computers we now use were designed.

Unfortunately, there is not space to pursue this exciting subject further, but it is worth mentioning that even within the very brief period computers have existed, they have been taught to play incredible games of chess; they have derived elegant solutions to complex logical problems; they have been used to compose music and even write poetry. So the question that must be raised is: 'How could so-called *intelligent* computers be employed in art and design?' Possible future scenarios might find computers in the twenty-first century advising on colour schemes, preparing a series of 2D layouts from a design brief, the automatic layout of images and text for books, developing families of patterns based on initial themes, or even proposing hundreds of ways of laying out 3D interiors.

There is every possibility that the computer of the future will become a valuable assistant to tomorrow's designer. It will acquire a wealth of design knowledge, be a source of creative ideas, and hopefully, a colleague with whom one can talk over any aspect of design.

CONCLUSION

Whether one can accept some of the futuristic ideas expressed above is not very important. It is important, however, to recognize that we are in the midst of a technological revolution; one that is already having a dramatic impact on the world of art and design. The preceding chapters attempted to reveal the success being achieved across a broad range of application areas and to demonstrate that at last computer technology has something substantial to offer designers and artists alike.

Glossary

8-bit colour Implies that 1 byte (8 bits) is associated with one pixel which permits the display of 256 grey levels or colours.

24-bit colour Implies that 3 bytes (24 bits) are associated with one pixel which permits the display of 16.7 million colours.

32-bit colour In 32-bit colour systems 24 bits are normally assigned to representing colour information while the remaining 8 bits are used as an alpha channel for masking operations in photomontage operations.

Additive primary colours The three colours: red, green and blue, which, when mixed in the form of light sources can match another single colour.

Adobe Type Manager (ATM) A software facility marketed by Adobe which derives bitmapped fonts for screen display from font descriptions used for laser printers.

Airbrush An air-driven painting device used to create photo-realistic images. Airbrush is also a painting mode on electronic painting systems for imitating traditional airbrushing.

Algorithm A precise specification for describing a solution to a problem; it is usually composed of a finite number of steps. For example, an algorithm is needed in computer programming to sort a set of numbers into ascending sequence.

Aliasing (a)Spatial aliasing describes artefacts such as jagged edges and moiré patterns caused by under-sampling an image.
(b)Temporal aliasing relates to effects like 'wagon wheels' apparently rotating backwards when filmed.

Alpha channel Used for storing stencils (mattes) for compositing images. It is normally 8 bits deep and enables the use of soft-edge stencils for minimizing edge artefacts.

Ambient light The constant illumination level associated with all surfaces; it is equivalent to light reaching the surface from all directions.

Analogue signal A signal that varies continuously without any discrete steps.

Animation The technique of creating continuous movement by projecting a series of discrete images in rapid succession.

Anti-aliasing In general, anti-aliasing describes techniques for minimizing the aliasing artefacts introduced by under-sampling.

AppleTalk Apple Macintosh's low-cost local area network.

Ascender A typographic term describing the portion of a lower-case letter that extends above the x-height of a letter, as in b, d, h, k, l, and t.

ASCII An acronym for the American Standard Code for Information Interchange which describes a 7-bit code for representing characters stored within a computer.

Aspect ratio The ratio of the vertical to the horizontal dimensions of an image. In television, the aspect ratio is 3:4, but the recommended ratio for high definition television is 9:16.

ATM See Adobe Type Manager.

Auto-dimensioning A feature of a CAD system where distances between two points are automatically computed when scaling operations are made or the points are repositioned.

Back painting The term given to the colouring of cels in animation; the back of the cel is painted rather than the front.

Bar sheets Used in animation for relating dialogue, music and character movement with frame numbers.

Baseline A typographic term for a reference line upon which letters are placed.

Bézier curve A smooth curve derived from three or more control points. While the curve always intersects the first and last points, it is only influenced by the positions of the other points. Bézier curves are used in computer graphics systems for describing smooth outline shapes, especially in font design.

Bézier surface patch Employs a matrix of points in space to control the surface geometry of a small patch of space. It is often used in CAD systems for describing the surface of a free-form object.

Billion In computer terminology, billion means one thousand million.

Binary A number system having two states, used in computers for encoding instructions and data. Our own number system is decimal as it employs ten states.

Bit Derived from BInary digiT, it is represented either by 1 or 0. Eight bits comprise one byte.

Bitmap An array of memory elements which when mapped directly to a display screen generates an image. For example, bitmaps are used for storing the character shapes displayed on a computer screen.

Bitmapping The technique of mapping an image stored in a computer's memory onto a display screen.

Boiling A term used in animation to describe the continuous movement seen in colours if cels have been manually airbrushed or rendered inconsistently.

Bump mapping A rendering technique where a photograph of rough material such as leather or stone is used to impart a bumpy surface to a computer-generated surface.

Byte A group of 8 bits of binary data.

CAD See Computer aided design.

Caption generator An electronic system for annotating broadcast TV pictures with text.

Cartesian coordinates Used in computer graphics for locating a point in 2D or 3D space. In 2D space a point requires two coordinates representing the horizontal and vertical distances from some arbitrary origin. In 3D space a point requires three similar values.

Cathode ray tube A television screen is a cathode ray tube, as it employs a scanning electron beam to excite the phosphor screen.

CCD See Charge coupled device.

Cel A thin sheet of transparent plastic upon which are painted the different layers of drawings in traditional cartoon animation.

Central processing unit (CPU) The vital part of a computer for executing the stored program of instructions.

Charge coupled device (CCD) A photosensitive cell which stores an electrostatic charge proportional to the incident illumination. A row of CCDs are used for scanning images in laser copiers.

Chooser Apple Macintosh's Desk Accessory for selecting a printer device connected to the AppleTalk network.

Chroma-key Describes a video technique for isolating a feature of an image by shooting a scene against a monochrome background – typically blue.

Chrominance Refers to the colour component of a television signal.

CLC Colour laser copier.

Clipping The process of removing those elements from the computer's world space that are invisible to the observer.

CMYK Cyan, magenta, yellow and a key colour, which is black.

Colour look-up table (LUT) A frame store may employ a colour look-up table to convert its internal codes into colour values.

Colour model A system used for describing the characteristics of colour. In computer graphics a colour can be described by additive components of red, green and blue (RGB) or the subtractive components of cyan, magenta and yellow (CMY). A colour can also be defined in terms of its hue, saturation and value (HSV).

Compiler A computer program for translating a program written in a high-level language such as Fortran, Pascal or C, into another which can be executed by a computer.

Compositing The process of creating an image from several separate images; usually achieved with the aid of a digital paint system.

Computer aided design (CAD) The application of computer systems for assisting the process of designing something. Such systems tend to employ computer graphics techniques.

Computer graphics Those applications of computers where images are manipulated and created.

Control vertex Bézier curves and surface patches use control vertices to influence their shape.

Coordinates The Cartesian coordinates of a point in 2D or 3D space are the offset distances from the origin.

CPU See Central processing unit.

CRT See Cathode ray tube.

Cut and paste A term used in word processing systems where part of the text can be 'cut' out of a document and 'pasted' in another position. It is also used in the context of images and sounds.

Database A method of organizing data hierarchically within a computer system.

Descender A typographic term for describing the portion of a lower-case letter that falls below the baseline, for example: g, j, p, q, and y.

Desktop publishing (DTP) A computer-based publishing facility implemented on a PC.

Diffuse reflector A surface which radiates reflected light in all directions. Consequently, its intensity is independent of the observer's position and only proportional upon the angle of the light source. It is an illumination model frequently employed in computer graphics.

Digital computer Uses a binary coding system for storing its program of instructions and data. The data may be numeric or alphabetic and the instructions perform arithmetic, input/output and logical operations.

Digitizer An active surface for generating Cartesian coordinates from line drawings.

Dithering Employs the scattering of different-sized dots to create a graduation of colour.

dpi Dots per inch.

Dragging A term associated with a WIMP environment, whereby a screen object is displaced from one position to another using a mouse.

DTP See Desktop publishing.

Easing The technique of altering the speed of an object when animated.

Environment mapping A rendering technique where an environment such as a room is mapped onto a computer-generated object to create a highly polished surface such as chrome.

Ethernet A fast local area network for connecting workstations and personal computers.

Extruding A modelling technique where a cross-section is extruded to develop a three-dimensional object.

Feather Synonomous with blending in a parameter or quality. For example, in photomontage, part of an image may be selected by a mask having a feathered edge. This graduated edge enables the image portion to be composited with another image without creating any obvious visual discontinuity.

File A collection of related records of data; for example, in computer graphics a 3D scene is stored as a file of coordinates.

Filter An image-processing operation for changing the quality of an image, such as blurring, pixelation or sharpening.

Floppy disk A small, flexible computer disk used for storing data. The two standard sizes are 3.5-inch and 5.25-inch.

Folder In a WIMP environment, a folder describes a sub-directory which in turn may hold other folders or files of data.

Font Another word for typeface. It describes a collection of symbols designed as an integrated family, such as Helvetica or Times.

Fractal The term was coined by Benoit Mandelbrot from the Latin *fractus* meaning 'broken' and is used to describe irregular data sets; these are used for texture maps and building mountainous terrains.

Frame grabbing The action of retrieving an image from a video camera. It is used in electronic paint systems for the input of live action images.

Frame store A memory device for storing a pixel-based image.

Free-form surface A term used for describing objects that have no obvious geometric symmetry, such as a teapot.

Gamma The relationship between the input signals forming a picture and the output intensity. This law is logarithmic and is often adjusted within computer graphics systems, and known as gamma correction.

Gamut In the context of colour computer graphics, gamut refers to the range of colours that are possible to display or manipulate within a system.

Gbyte 1,024 Mbyte of computer storage.

Gouraud shading A rendering technique where a surface is shaded by linearly interpolating colour values across a raster.

Graduation A subtle blend of intensity or colour from one tone to another.

Graphical user interface (GUI) A computer which uses graphical elements in a user interface. Apple Macintosh computers employ this method of allowing users to control the operating system and various application packages.

Graphics card A printed circuit board which can be added to a computer to provide an enhanced graphics facility.

Graph plotter A computer output peripheral for drawing line artwork from internally stored data.

Greeking A term used in printing, where Latin or Greek text is used to illustrate how sample pages of text will look when filled with information. It is also used to describe the use of grey bars to show the position of text on screen pages in DTP systems.

Greyscale The levels of grey that exist between black and white. When one byte is used to store these levels, 256 grey levels are possible.

GUI See Graphical user interface.

Halftone The halftone printing process uses a fine grid of dots to control the intensity of an image. For full-colour images four colour separations are made to represent the cyan, magenta, yellow and black components.

Hard disk A fixed disk associated with a computer as opposed to a flexible disk, which can be inserted and retrieved from the system.

Hardware A term for describing the physical components comprising a computer system.

HDTV See High definition television.

Headline font A font design specifically used for headlines, as scaled smaller fonts are not visually correct. Headline fonts tend not to be legible at text sizes.

Hidden-line removal The process of removing the edges from a scene that are potentially masked by other surfaces.

High definition television (HDTV) The proposed new standard for consumer television. It anticipates a resolution of over 1,000 lines and an aspect ratio of 9:16.

Hinting A process for ensuring that small bitmapped fonts are not distorted by the pixel sampling process when they are displayed.

Hue Any colour can be defined in terms of its hue, saturation and value. Hue describes the intrinsic colour component such as red, orange, yellow, green or blue.

Hz Cycles per second. It is derived from the name of the famous scientist Hertz, who pioneered the techniques of transmitting and receiving radio waves.

Icon A small graphic symbol representing a feature in a graphical user interface.

Image compression A technique for compressing an image file so that it takes up less storage space without losing any information.

Image processing Involves techniques that process a pixel-based image to enhance it in some way or extract a feature. For example, techniques exist for blurring or sharpening an image.

Image resolution The number of pixel samples

in an image. For example, this might be the number of horizontal and vertical pixels in a scanned image.

Imagesetter A laser-driven printing device for converting digital data onto photosensitive film. In the printing industry an imagesetter takes the output from an RIP to create the rasters that comprise all images.

Image sharpening An image enhancing process where pixel intensities are altered to create the impression that the image becomes sharper.

Interface The point where two separate systems communicate with one another. For example, humans communicate with computers through a computer-human interface, and a computer communicates with a printer via a parallel electrical interface.

Interlacing The technique of splitting a television image into two separate components called fields. The odd raster lines comprise one field and the even raster lines the other.

Interpolation A mathematical technique for computing an

intermediate value between two other values. In typography, an interpolated letter shape can be obtained from two other master shapes. In animation, inbetween frames can be interpolated from the parameters describing two other key frames.

Justification A typographic term describing the process of introducing spaces between words in lines of type to make left and right edges vertical and even.

Kbyte A kilobyte is 1,024 bytes of memory or disk storage.

Kerning A typographic term describing the optimum spaces used to position different pairs of characters.

Key frame In animation, key framing enables a sequence of animation to be developed from two or more key frames describing the status of various elements. The inbetween frames are computed by interpolating the parameters associated with the key frames.

Keying In video post production, keying is a process whereby two video signals are

proportionally mixed depending on the value of a key signal.

LAN See Local area network.

Laptop computer A small portable computer.

Lay planning In the fashion and textile industries, lay planning is the process of organizing the pattern elements on the final material to minimize wastage.

Leading A typographic term for measuring the distance between two neighbouring rows of text in units of points.

Local area network (LAN) A system for connecting together a number of computers so that they can communicate with one another. AppleTalk is a LAN.

Luminance The brightness component of a colour.

LUT See Colour look-up table.

Mbyte A 1K x 1K block of memory or disk storage. It is equivalent to 1,048,576 bytes.

Memory The part of a computer used for storing the program of instructions.

Menu A list of actions or parameters a user may choose from when working with a WIMP environment.

MIPS Millions of Instructions Per Second.

Modelling The process of constructing two- or three-dimensional elements within a computer environment.

Moiré An unwanted interference pattern that can arise when regular textures are displayed upon a television screen, or when halftone colour separation grids are not rotated correctly to one another. In general, if yellow is rotated through 90°, then cyan is rotated through 105°, magenta 75°, and black 45°.

Monochrome An image formed from one colour: it is typically used for describing black-and-white images.

Mouse A hand-held device associated with most modern computers and is used for controlling the position of a screen cursor.

NTSC The National Television Standards Committee: the American television standard.

Operating system A program resident in a computer to enable the machine to be controlled easily.

Outline font A font description where Beziér curves are used to define the outline shapes.

Paint system An interactive computer where the user is allowed to create a coloured image without the use of conventional painting materials.

PAL Phase Alternate Line: the UK television standard.

Palette In electronic paint systems, a palette is the collection of colours employed by the user.

PC Personal Computer.

PDL See Page Description Language.

Persistence (a) A phosphor's ability to continue glowing after it is no longer being excited.
(b) The retina's ability to remain excited after it has been stimulated.

Phong shading A rendering technique developed by Bui Tuong Phong which incorporates specular highlights.

Pica A typographic measurement meaning 12 points and is equal to about 4 millimetres.

Pixel The smallest addressable element of a picture. This might be the individual pixels on a display screen or the individual points sampled on a physical image.

Point A typographic unit of measurement used with metal type, equivalent to approximately 1/72nd of an inch. The term is still used to define the height of characters in many DTP systems.

Polygon A shape formed from a chain of straight edges.

Post-production Encompasses all the procedures needed to integrate the many individual sequences that make up a final piece of video.

PostScript A Page Description Language developed by Adobe, which has virtually become a *de facto* standard on the Macintosh range of computers.

Primary colours A primary colour implies that it cannot be composed from other colours in the colour model. For example, in the RGB scheme, red is a primary colour as it cannot be created by mixing together green and blue.

Pseudo-colouring The process of allocating false colours to an image.

Radiosity A global illumination model used for rendering highly realistic images using the diffuse light intensities arising from multiple reflections encountered in interiors.

RAM See Random access memory.

Random access memory (RAM) The memory used in a computer for storing a program and its data. It can be read from as well as written to.

Raster One line of pixels displayed on a television or a computer display screen.

Raster graphics Computer graphics systems which process images formed from rasters of pixels.

Raster image processor (RIP) A computer which converts a PDL file into a raster format for output to an imagesetter.

Ray tracing A technique for rendering 3D images by tracing the rays of light which effectively arrive at the individual screen pixels. The technique is useful for deriving specular reflections, shadows and refractions.

Read only memory (ROM) A block of memory which can only be read from and not written to, as in the case of RAM. It is often used to store a program which is automatically loaded into a computer.

Rendering The process of creating an image from an internal description of a scene.

RGB Red, green and blue.

RIP See Raster image processor.

ROM See Read only memory.

Sampling The process of converting an analogue signal into a digital signal. For example, a photograph which basically represents a continuum of colour must be sampled at discrete points to convert it into a digital format.

Saturation When a colour is described in terms of hue, saturation and value, saturation describes the degree of white light contained in the colour.

Scanner A device for converting an image stored on paper or film into a matrix of pixels. Some scanners can reduce an image into its three primary colour components.

Screen angles The four angles through which the halftone colour separations must be rotated to minimize moiré patterns.

Separations To output a full-colour image from a computer for printing, four colour separations are required in terms of the cyan, yellow, magenta, and black components.

Soft edge A term associated with a stencil whose boundary is represented by many levels of intensity and which enables perfect montage effects to be obtained.

Software A generic term for computer programs.

Spatial aliasing See Aliasing.

Specular reflection Associated with polished surfaces. It refers to the phenomenon whereby an observer can see reflections of light sources in a surface.

Stylus A hand-held pen used in conjunction with an interactive tablet.

Subtractive primary colours The colours cyan, yellow and magenta which, when combined as printing inks, can be used to match another single colour. However, black is introduced into the printing process to guarantee that a rich black level is achieved.

System 7 Macintosh's current Operating System.

Tablet A small digitizing surface.

Temporal aliasing See Aliasing.

Texture map A source of texture, perhaps a photograph, to be used in a texture mapping operation.

Texture mapping A method of increasing the realism of a computer-generated image by covering it with some source of real or synthetic texture.

Tint A wash of colour using a halftone process, which introduces colour as a matrix of fine dots in a printing process.

Transistor A small semi-conductor device capable of controlling an electrical current. In computers, transistors are used to perform the binary switching operations.

Undo command Allows the user to return to the computer's status before the last command was issued.

UNIX A computer operating system.

Value Any colour can be defined in terms of its hue, saturation and value. Value measures its lightness or darkness between the limits of black and white.

Vector graphics Relates to computer images composed from a series of discrete lines (vectors), as opposed to raster graphics which forms an image from a regular collection of horizontal rasters of pixels.

Vertex Identifies the end point of a 2D line or 3D edge.

VGA Video Graphics Array, developed by IBM for the PS/2 computer. Its standard resolution is 640 x 480 but it can be extended to 1,024 x 768.

It can display 256 colours from a palette of 256K.

Video card A printed circuit board which converts a computer's digital circuits into a video format for recording purposes.

Video signal Encodes the chrominance and luminance information of a raster image together with the synchronization pulses controlling the display device.

Vignette See Graduation.

Virtual reality A method of interfacing a user to a 3D interactive computer graphic environment. A full implementation may involve a stereoscopic head-mounted display and a glove fitted with transducers to detect finger flexions, where both the user's head and hand are tracked in space and in real time.

Virus Malicious people write programs called viruses which cause havoc in computer systems.

The virus finds its way into a computer system when software is copied from 'infected' disks, and can remain dormant for many years. When activated by the computer's clock, the virus program can destroy files or prevent the computer from working correctly.

VLSI Very Large Scale Integration. It is associated with the manufacture of silicon chips.

WIMP Windows, Icons, Mouse and Pointer. It is associated with a GUI as found on Macintosh computers.

Window A rectangular area of a display screen where a user can control some independent computer task.

Wireframe A term used to describe a view of an object where all the edges are drawn, making it seem as if the object was constructed from wire.

World space An imaginary 3D space employed in computer graphics where a virtual observer, objects and light sources are located.

WYSIWYG What You See Is What You Get. Generally means that what one sees upon a display screen is what will be printed upon a hard-copy device.

X-height A typographic term measuring the height of the main body of a letter such as the letter x.

YUV A colour model used in PAL television signals where Y is the luminance, and U and V are the colour difference values.

Bibliography

Badler, Barsky and Zeltzer (Eds) (1990) *Making them Move – Mechanics, Control and Animation of Articulated Figures.* Morgan Kaufmann Publishers: Hove. (Video and book.)

Booth-Clibborn, E and Poyner, R (1991) *Typography Now.* Booth-Clibborn Editions: London. Distributed by Internos Books.

Burke, C (1991) *Type from the Desktop: Designing with Type and your Computer.* Ventana Press Inc: North Carolina.

Foley, van Dam, Feiner and Hughes (1990) *Computer Graphics: Principles and Practice.* Addison-Wesley: Wokingham.

Frutiger, A (1991) *The International Type Book.* Van Nostrand Reinhold: Kentucky.

Hinrichs, K and Hirasuna, D (1991) *Typewise.* North Light Books: Ohio.

Katsui, M and Kawahara, T (Eds) (1991) *World Graphic Design – Computer Graphics Vol 6.* Kodansha: Tokyo.

McCullough, M, Mitchell, W and Purcell, P (1990) *The Electronic Design Studio: Architectural Knowledge and Media in the Computer Era.* MIT Press: Cambridge, Mass.

Mealing, S (1992) *The Art and Science of Computer Animation.* Intellect: London.

Merritt, D (1987) *Television Graphics: From Pencil to Pixel.* Trefoil: London.

Pipes, A (Ed) (1986) *Computer-Aided Architectural Design Futures.* Butterworth: Guildford.

Pipes, A (1990) *Drawing for 3-dimensional Design.* Thames & Hudson: London.

Pipes, A (1992) *Production for Graphic Designers.* Prentice-Hall: New York.

Stone, S (1991) *The Art and Use of Typography on the Personal Computer.* Bedford Arts: California.

Sun Microsystems Inc. (1992) *An Introduction to Computer Graphics Concepts.* Addison-Wesley: Wokingham.

Todd, S and Latham, W (1992) *Evolutionary Art and Computers.* Academic Press: London.

Vince, J (1990) *The Language of Computer Graphics.* ADT Press: London.

Vince, J (1992) *3D Computer Animation.* Addison-Wesley: Wokingham.

Watt, A and Watt, M (1992) *Advanced Animation and Rendering Techniques.* Addison-Wesley: Wokingham.

Weinstock, N (1991) *Computer Animation.* Addison-Wesley: Wokingham.

PERIODICALS

Art & Design. Academy Group Ltd, USA.

Art in America. Brant Art Publications Inc, USA.

Communication Arts. Coyne & Blanchard Inc, USA.

Computer Graphics & Applications. The IEEE Computer Society, USA.

Creative Review. Centaur Communications Ltd, UK.

Design. The Design Council, UK.

Domus. Editoriale Domus spa, USA.

Graphics World. Datateam Publishing Ltd, UK.

Leonardo. Pergammon Press, UK.

Print. RC Publications Inc, USA.

Seybold Report on Publishing Systems. Seybold Publications Inc, USA.

Visualization and Computer Animation. John Wiley & Sons Ltd, UK.

Index